THE UNSEEN SHORE

THE
UNSEEN
SHORE

Memories
of a Christian Science Childhood

THOMAS SIMMONS

BEACON PRESS
BOSTON

Beacon Press
25 Beacon Street
Boston, Massachusetts 02108

Beacon Press books
are published under the auspices of
the Unitarian Universalist Association of Congregations.

98 97 96 95 94 93 92 91   8 7 6 5 4 3 2 1

Text design by Ruth Kolbert

Library of Congress Cataloging-in-Publication Data

Simmons, Thomas, 1956–
The unseen shore : memories of a Christian Science childhood /
Thomas Simmons.
p.   cm.
ISBN 0-8070-1018-9
1. Simmons, Thomas, 1956– . 2. Christian Scientists—United
States—Biography. I. Title.
BX6996.S48A3 1991
289.5'092—dc20
[B]   90-22936
CIP

FOR
Nathaniel
and
Georgia

ACKNOWLEDGMENTS

I wish to thank the Reverend Cynthia Bourgeault and Professor John Simmons, my sister and brother, for going over the old family territory with me; they saved me from some important errors of fact. The office of the clerk of the First Church of Christ, Scientist in Los Altos, California, the reference staff of the Palo Alto Public Library, the service department of Belmont Volkswagen in Belmont, Massachusetts, and Jeanne Geselschap have all been helpful in confirming or correcting my memories of specific events. None of these individuals or organizations, of course, is in any way responsible for my interpretations of the past.

My copy editor, Chris Kochansky, gave the manuscript meticulous care, for which I am most grateful. I am grateful as well to the editorial and marketing staff of Beacon Press, whose expertise cheered me as I brought this project to a close.

Lauren Bryant, my editor at Beacon, first saw the promise in this manuscript. Her foresight and editorial acumen have enabled me to publish a book which ultimately affirms all that is strong and sustaining in my life. To her I offer my deepest thanks.

T.S.

Belmont, Massachusetts
October 1990

CONTENTS

There is no life, truth, intelligence, nor substance in matter. All is infinite Mind and its infinite manifestation, for God is All-in-all. Spirit is immortal Truth; matter is mortal error. Spirit is the real and eternal; matter is the unreal and temporal. Spirit is God, and man is His image and likeness. Therefore man is not material; he is spiritual.

–MARY BAKER EDDY,
"The Scientific Statement of Being"

And as they were eating, Jesus took bread, and blessed it, and brake it, and gave it to the disciples, and said, Take, eat; this is my body.

–MATTHEW 26:26

PREFACE

ANY PLACE WILL DO, I HAVE ALWAYS TOLD MYSELF, BUT SOME
places are better than others. This place, for instance. To begin
with, it is an island. There are no roads to this island, no
bridges. The twelve-car ferry runs six times a day in the
summer, and when it is out (as it was last week—radar
failure), the eight-car ferry is substituted. If you want to get
on and off the island with any regularity, you have to work
at it. There is a nurse on the island, and two fire trucks, and
an ambulance, but no doctor. The ferry stays at the island
slip at night in case of emergencies: the town selectmen can
authorize a midnight run to the mainland for medical reasons.

From the ferry slip I drive my car about a half-mile down
a narrow road, turn left, then left again, and drive along a
pair of gravel ruts until I come to one of the two official island
cemeteries. Then I turn right into a dirt driveway. The house
facing me there, behind the stand of spruces, is my sister's
house. It is not home exactly, but it is a place to go.

The front door with its heavy winter weatherstripping lets go with a loud suctiony sound as I push it open. To my left, the kitchen; to my right, the dining room; straight ahead, the living room and woodburning stove. Everything here is expected, unsurprising. The stairway goes up one flight to the two bedrooms and the bathroom. From there a narrow set of stairs—almost incidental, like attic stairs—twists up to this room where I am now sitting.

In the time I have written this the sky has moved from dusk to night. The pale eaves reflect the navy blue sky exactly, so that inner and outer begin to blur. Only the frame of the skylight marks the difference, and it seems to float above me, not apparitional, but clean and precise.

I am sitting at a desk with a word processor, and now that the day has faded, the only light in the room comes from my screen, where the new lines of words add an appreciable glow, like a night light or a rank of runway lights at a familiar airport. Familiar words, familiar glow. The words and light wrap around me like a second room. A sanctuary. This is a place to begin.

But to begin what? Here, three hundred miles from home, I tend to do more or less what I do at home: look after my young son Nathaniel, buy groceries, drive the garbage to the dump, wash the car. Now, near the end of the day, I have only the feeling that I have done nothing, nothing—and this in spite of everything that I have done, everything dutiful and kind and even joyful. At night the emptiness sets in. And that is why I am here—to confront this emptiness, so common that I mostly seem to carry it around with me like a shadow self. What am I looking for? What is better, or more real, than nothingness?

In the darkness, things begin to separate themselves and become discrete, dark objects in a darker space. Above my head, next to the skylight, I can still make out the glint of ice in a photograph of a tree in winter. This is actually a small poster, almost entirely dark except for a glossy streak of ambient twilight across the ice. There is a quotation on the photo,

now invisible, which comes from Camus. Like many such
quotations, lifted out of context and lacking a crescendo or a
trailing off, it seems quite ordinary. "In the midst of winter,"
it says, "I finally learned that there was within me an invin-
cible summer." I stare at the darkness where the quotation
is, thinking. This was the poster that hung over my mother's
bed in the last few weeks of her life, when she was dying of
cancer. That was ten years ago. I had no idea the poster was
still around, but my sister must have rescued it, and here it
is again, in the attic room of her house. I am alone, and still
the presence of the family looms above me like a dark angel,
or a distant star.

The family is one place to begin. In this room it encircles
my emptiness like a shroud around a crèche. As I look along
the length of the attic, I see in the halo of a near window the
baroque, papier-mâché angel my mother hung from her window in the Christian Science care home where she died. The
shape is both precise and florid: this is Gabriel, whose robe
sweeps down in the rush of his ascent, and whose wings flare
out sharply like a hawk's. When it first appeared, hanging by
a thread from the curtain rod in my mother's room, I thought
of it as a bit of comic relief—a touch of the Catholicism my
mother disdained to lighten the heavy burden of her own
faith. She trusted that the religion in which she had spent her
life would heal her of this dreadful and terrifying disease. By
the time the angel appeared, it seemed that this miracle would
not occur. And so, over the next few weeks, her last weeks,
I came to understand the angel as something more intimate
than a joke. It was a kind of three-dimensional hallucination
for my mother as she came in and out of consciousness. It
was her final friend, her closest and truest companion. We,
her children, came and went, we prayed, we hoped, we sat
in silence, we wept, we wearied her. But the garish angel
stayed, defying with its ugliness all the aesthetic and intellectual beauty my mother had cherished through her religion
for more than fifty years. The faith it embodied became physical and actual. In the end my mother had a Virgil for her

Dantesque journey into the darkness. And that angel is with me now, although I thought it too had been lost.

When I was a child, I went to a Sunday school where the Lord's Prayer was taught with a correlative reading. (This was a kind of commentary built right into the text.) Near the beginning of each Sunday meeting, the children would recite the lines from the Lord's Prayer, and the Sunday school superintendent would recite the commentary from Mary Baker Eddy's *Science and Health with Key to the Scriptures*. "Our Father, which art in heaven," we would begin, and then we'd pause, waiting for the superintendent to read her line from the book. "Our Father-Mother God," she would say, "all-harmonious." From the age of two and a half, when I first arrived in Sunday school, to the age of twenty, when I left, I heard these words—"Father-Mother God." These should have been words of comfort, and sometimes they were: we were not orphans; our heavenly parents looked out upon us from their spiritual reality, which was everywhere, and guided us with a love greater than any human being could imagine. There was no stern lawgiver, no intimidating patriarchal presence. The emphasis was not on male and female, but on father and mother, the dual guardians of the ideal family.

We all—most of us—had both fathers and mothers. We knew what they did in our families. In Sunday school we learned to move from our own fathers and mothers to their divine source. This must have seemed, to our teachers, to be an appropriate way of introducing us to God: He and She were like our parents, only more so. There were difficulties, of course, which we were not expected to notice, at least not as young children; when we did notice them, they made our teachers stutter or stumble. Mother and father were one in Christian Science, but in our lives they were two; mother and father were abstract in Christian Science—discussed in terms of their spiritual synonyms, Life, Truth, and Love—but in our lives they were real people, with very distinct characters and behaviors. Dad and Mom became useful examples for

the teaching of divine faith, because together they symbolized
the completeness of the universe as well as the loving immanence of God. Yet what sometimes underlay this completeness on earth was not perfect love, but anger, misery,
and want.

In this way my religion seemed inextricably bound up with
my family when I was a child. The Father-Mother I met every
Sunday morning was my father and my mother, who somehow were extended into a realm of immense power and
light—and love. This was an awful magnification. I wondered: did the Father-Mother God have the explosive silences
of my father and mother, and how were they magnified? Did
the sky thunder, as it seemed to in my house, when God
could no longer keep His silence? And if He spoke simply in
rages or benedictions, thunder or warm sun, then why did
we speak in words at all? What could we possibly say that
would alter the ultimate rages or blessings of God?

My teachers being emphatic about the love of the Father-
Mother God, I could not explain to them how I had seen
another side of the divine Face. These were my own nightmares, they said, or—when I grew more used to the termi-
nology of Christian Science—the brash workings of mortal
mind: I should dismiss such errant thoughts, and trust in God
to ease my fears. But in my heart of hearts I always heard
God speaking with two voices, the one deep, the other high
and volatile. For years it seemed that I could do nothing but
wait for the two voices to become one—or find in their division a new power.

What was curious about the Father-Mother God was the
neat and closed universe it provided in spite of my divided
perceptions. God's world was my world; my family's world
was God's world. We were united. And in this unity we
achieved a kind of static perfection; the context of our world
never changed. As long as we accepted God's love, nothing
could ever happen to our family that would harm our relationship with God, and nothing would ever happen to God.
The facts of our experience were permanent—God the father

and mother, God the family—and this somehow evolved into an assurance that nothing would ever be radically different from the normal and comfortable state into which I was born.

This, at any rate, was what I learned both in Sunday school and from my mother, who worked hard to preserve the church teachings in me and ultimately became herself the superintendent of the Sunday school. I was a child of God; I was perfect; I lived in a world of love and light. Any perceptions I had that were contrary to these facts were false, the mischievous deceptions of mortal mind. Mortal mind was the shadow mind, the unreality posing as reality or the un-God posing as God. My security arose from my right thinking. Knowing myself to be a perfect child of God, I made my life inviolable. I could relax; I was safe.

And yet, I saw, I was not safe. My mother, who was telling me of Father-Mother God's perfection, was herself suffering—prone to angry silences, resentful, exhausted, and full of a longing I could not understand for years. My father, the other component of this static perfection, traveled frequently and returned half-grateful, half-hateful of all that we represented. The family was his refuge and his prison: my brother and sister and I knew this from his first hug and his first fury at something we had done in his absence. Could mortal mind invade even God? And could the emissaries of God on earth suffer so within the immutable context of love that God had established for them like an eternal Garden of Eden? Evidently they did suffer, but we could not admit this. Mortal mind was, technically, nothing, but it was real enough to any child who crept halfway down the stairs to watch a family fight, and so became a translucent, de facto devil.

The only escape, as years passed, seemed to be flight—utter freedom, rejecting the static perfection and the father and the mother. But when both father and mother were images of God, what could freedom be? And—worse yet—if sex was the progenitor of mother and father, then the static universe collapsed, and one had nothing to rebel against, because what had been so perfect and reliable was itself unreal. God was unreal.

Peace. Truce. The thoughts from years past, disorganized and clamorous, crowd back like a guerrilla band. How long have I been sitting here, thinking and writing? I can't remember. The alarm clock at my side stopped some time ago—dead batteries, or perhaps no one has bothered to plug it in. My mind idles. Now, at least for a few minutes, there is all time—time to stretch, to recover the present and its comforts. One thing and another: I am back there, in the tides of the past, but I am also here, in my sister's house on this beautiful island, and here is my anchor.

What I had, as a child, was a world of language—a world in which all was good, and in which evil was a deception, a form of non-existence. If I have become in some ways deeply suspicious of language, it is in part because I grew up knowing how easily a seemingly clear and liberating statement—for example, "I think, therefore I am"—could mean something murky and entangling, a kind of bargain. In my religion, "I think, therefore I am" meant "I think, therefore I am purely spiritual"; that reasoning entailed serious consequences. If I wanted the security of a clearly defined universe, such as Christian Science offered, I also had to take the rigid context, in which unreality and reality were as clear and artificial as night and day in a cave. Seeing this finally, feeling it, I began to fight for an escape. I wanted absolute freedom, in which I might start over and become new. It did not happen. What I found, instead, was emptiness, with a conventional life to distract me from the emptiness. And now, having seen emptiness as the enemy, I have turned to face it.

But perhaps it is not the enemy, or at least not such an enemy as I have been making it out to be. What I have found in facing this void is that it places me on unstable ground, where nothing is secure and no orthodoxy comes to my aid—not religion, not psychology, not art, not science. Yet what I have lacked all these years, I think, is a willingness to concede that the unstable may be good, or at least useful. I have lived most of my life in a world of rigid contexts, and I have sought to leave one for another and another. It has not worked. What I have not tried is a journey that presumes no context at all— that trusts, in fact, not in a stable reality, but in an unstable one.

The morning ferry that leaves tomorrow will leave with my family and me aboard. This place is peaceful and wild and far away; nevertheless after seven hours of driving we will be back in Boston, in the heart of everything that has emerged from the confused tangle of certainties and misunderstandings that comprises my life. I have not done much here, but I have begun to set out a route through emptiness. I will not turn back if I can help it.

I

CRUELTY

OUR MEMORIES OF PAINFUL EXPERIENCES USUALLY RECEDE over time. This is generally a good thing: it allows us to get on with living, even as we try to make some sense of what caused the pain. Sometimes, though, the pain stays; only a slight tug at the threads of memory can call it back in its dark mundanity.

Now, almost without effort, I transport myself back to the child I was at four or five or six, writhing in pain on my bed. It is early evening. The dull ache that started to annoy my left ear several hours ago now blazes through my head. I cannot rest. Every motion is agony, but lying still is impossible. When I try to calm myself, I feel the pain boring into my brain like a fusillade of needles. The fever I have had for hours covers my body in sweat. I clench and unclinch my hands, I kick my feet, I scream. From past experience I know this will go on all night, possibly longer. But time scarcely has any meaning: each second is consumed in fire.

Even now I can feel traces of this pain creeping up the side of my neck. It's a prickly, anxious feeling. What I had then, of course, was an ear infection. Many kids get them regularly. To be free of this infection, one goes to a doctor who prescribes amoxicillin, known as the bubble-gum medicine because it's often given to young children in a liquid form that tastes just like bubble gum. The medicine gives quick relief; children usually take it for seven to ten days, except in more severe cases when a prophylactic dose may subsequently be prescribed. I know this because my own son Nathaniel periodically has ear infections. More than once in the middle of the night we have freed him from his pain by going to an urgent care clinic for bubble-gum medicine.

When I was a child, however, I was not freed from this pain. I did not go to a doctor. I did not receive amoxicillin or any other antibiotic. What I received instead was the extraordinary, elastic kindness of my mother, who stayed up with me all night when I was writhing in bed. As Christian Scientists we did not go to doctors. When I began to feel feverish and miserable, when my ear rang with pain and the flesh around it swelled angrily, my mother would telephone a Christian Science practitioner who would pray for her. (Because Mary Baker Eddy affirmed that a child's illness needed to be treated "mainly through the parent's thought," practitioners prayed primarily for the parents of a sick child rather than for the child.) Although instantaneous healings were part of the lore of Christian Science—I heard about them regularly in Sunday school—I do not remember being instantaneously healed of any ear infection, or even being healed at all. I remember hours and hours of unrelieved pain—and my mother, who did everything she could to comfort me.

Any parent knows the kind of sacrifice required to nurse a sick child through the night. Exhausted from worry and from lack of sleep, my mother would nevertheless hold me in her arms and sing hymns. In her small voice, with its keen, flat intonation, she would work her way through the seven original hymns of Mary Baker Eddy, and then move on to others I liked—Christmas carols, Easter songs, the doxology. And when my cries became too distracting, she would give up being the passive witness of God's healing power and do something on her own. She would fill a heavy old woolen sock with salt, heat it in the oven, and place it over my ear. The heat from the sock would briefly ease my pain, and for a few minutes I would know a minor, delirious peace. How she reconciled this recourse to material aids—wool, salt, heat—with her belief in unadulterated spiritual healing was never clear to me. But fundamentally it makes perfect, simple sense. She was a mother. Her child was suffering. She understood her religion to preclude seeking medical relief for his suffering. Desperate, she used whatever tools—material and spiritual—were at hand.

Because my mother was an immensely kind woman, it seems grotesque to suggest that she was also cruel. Can a son ever say, really, that his mother is cruel? It sounds spiteful or blasphemous at first; on second thought it merely seems irrelevant. And yet, at least in this case, it is not irrelevant. The cruelty my mother inflicted on me, and on my brother and sister, was scarcely intentional, and the power of her love should have reassured us that we were precious in her sight. From a very early age, however, we all knew that we were suffering unnecessarily, cruelly. "The opposite of cruelty is not kindness," says the philosopher Philip Hallie. "The opposite of cruelty is freedom. The victim does not need the ultimately destructive gift of kindness when offered within the cruel relationship. He needs freedom from that relationship." My mother's kindness was genuine, but it did not change the cruelty. What we needed was freedom from a cruel relationship, but this was impossible. For behind my mother and father stood the church and its parental God, which enchained us with its freedom.

Of course we were free—that was the whole point of our faith. We were free from the tyranny of believing in the reality of mortal existence. We were free from the tyranny of the body, which Christian Science showed to be a false conception of the perfect man. We were free from hunger, loneliness, bereavement, and every other kind of lack or want because in reality we already possessed everything we could possibly need. All we had to do was to open ourselves to God's perfection—to pray and believe—and we would see all around us the gifts we already had.

There was a catch, of course. The power of the mortal world, or mortal mind, was negligible, but this world seemed powerful to us humans, and when we were slow to fight this "error" it would appear in our lives as sickness, injury, hatefulness, envy, misery, death. The more we consented to an erroneous view of the world, the farther we were from God. I remember very clearly several occasions when Sunday school teachers would warn us that medical doctors were not to be trusted because the world they believed in was not our world—it was the world of mortal mind, of disease and distress. The only way to avoid this world, which seemed so pervasive, was to deny its reality resolutely whenever it appeared to us. When we were sick, we did not call a doctor; we prayed to know the fact of our perfect health. In this way, from a very young age, we were free of the common reality. "Be of good cheer," said Jesus, "for I have overcome the world." That was what we were to do as well; that was our freedom.

And so, lying in bed all those nights with ear infections, I was free. I was free through all of my innumerable colds and fevers, and I was free when at the age of three I walked in front of a moving metal swing that tore a jagged gash in my forehead. I was free when, in third grade, I had bronchitis for three weeks. (Unable to eat without vomiting, I grew so emaciated that my mother carried me off in desperation to a doctor, who shook his head with incredulity at the delay and gave me the antibiotics that cured me.) Because I was free (I was reminded regularly in Sunday school), I was not to question the extent of my suffering; the suffering was simply unreal. In the depths of the night, when I screamed and writhed from some disease, what I seemed to need most were my mother's comfort and kindness and prayers; these were extensions of God on earth, and would separate me from my false belief in pain. Eventually I would come to realize the freedom from pain that, in spiritual terms, I already possessed.

How well we all learned these lessons, my brother and sister and I! And yet, after an illness, the memory of the cruelty and the suffering did not simply go away. It lingered, an evil, competing reality, raising an insistent complaint: was the pain really unreal? Was it necessary to endure so much? Sitting in a rocking chair on the porch of our house in Pennsylvania, weak after a day or a week or a month of illness, I heard these questions but could not answer them. It was as if my mind drew a blank when they crossed it: there was simply no place for them in my reality. And because I could not deal with them, I could not escape.

HAVE I ESCAPED NOW? ENORMOUS QUESTION—WHO KNOWS? The obvious answer is Yes, of course I've escaped. I now go to doctors; I no longer lie for helpless hours in bed, writhing and trying to pray. I take medicine. And I am glad when the medicine works quickly, as it usually does. I am glad to know that intelligent people have devoted their lives to understanding physiology and biochemistry and pharmacology, so that other human beings—including my children and I—might be relieved of suffering.

I do not underestimate the significance of this change in my behavior. My mother could spend her whole life giving other names to cruelty, but I could not. And yet I am my mother's son: what she taught me, and what I learned in church, was not simply a matter of behavior. It was a matter of belief, of faith.

Despite my suffering, I firmly believed for many years that God would regularly enter my life and transform it. I believed I would be healed, even when I was not healed. And that faith invaded and sustained my entire life. If it was a cruel faith, many kind people along the way encouraged me to remain faithful—Sunday school teachers, practitioners, colleagues on the *Christian Science Monitor* when I worked there as an intern. When I began to tug against the confines of this faith, the fear of the physical world—and of doctors—always brought me back. Did I really want to live in a world where people went into hospitals, had operations, lived for days or weeks with tubes coming out of their bodies, died miserably? That was the world of mortal mind; I had been offered entry into the world beyond mortal mind. Didn't I want to stay in that world beyond—even if it wasn't quite as perfect as everyone made it out to be?

I did, I did. Perhaps I still do. And that edge of doubt, that distrust of freedom, is what makes me wonder if I have escaped. The elastic bubble of my family and my religion still surrounds me, stretching as I pull away, giving a little each time—tearing a little—but still stretching. And then, of course, there's the old linguistic problem: since by my old standards I was never anything *but* free, I cannot need freedom now.

One of the functions of language is to disguise the fact that we have no alternatives. The kinds of words we have for home, for example, and the ways we have of thinking about this place and state of mind, may disguise brilliantly the underlying cruelty of a particular home. Home is a safe harbor, a castle where we can raise the proverbial drawbridge, a locus of love and peace. When I think quickly of home, I think of our old brick house in Pennsylvania, where I played in the snow and had hot chocolate after Sunday school and snuck down the back stairs like a secret agent. I love this place; it can almost bring tears to my eyes.

When I look more closely, however, I can see myself writhing in pain from earaches, and I can see my mother on the telephone to practitioners who could not heal me. I can see, slowly, the seam beginning to show in the almost seamless relationship between home and mother and father and the

Father-Mother God. They were *not* all one. God was not in the room with me—at least not the God I knew from the words of Christian Science. He was somewhere else, waiting for me to become me—waiting for that long, long process to begin. He was waiting for my mother as well, and I began to see that He left her clues about what she should do to start on the road to His presence. But she would not, could not start: her own family, her own sense of home, and the very religion that promised to bring her close to God prevented her from taking more than a few stumbling steps toward Him.

I feel ill at ease writing these words, but that is how it seems to me. How cruel home was! Not for me alone, but for my mother, and for my father, and for my brother and sister as well. But now, as the seams begin to show, I can find some breathing room. For years I believed that home was the free world, the domain of God and love, and the world beyond was a wilderness. Yet the wilderness, I remind myself, was a place to begin: John the Baptist found wild honey there.

WHEN I WAS EIGHT, MY SIXTEEN-YEAR-OLD BROTHER JOHN SHOT out the windows of our neighbor's sunporch with his BB gun. He had learned how to shoot at a Christian Science summer camp, and his talent as a marksman impressed the camp counselors; they wrote encouraging reports to my parents, who supported his interest in shooting when he returned. In this way he remained true to his chosen route of escape—rebellion—even if it didn't work very well. I thought he showed restraint with the neighbor's windows; he could, after all, have used his .22 or his twelve-gauge shotgun, either of which would have caused considerably more damage. But no one else seemed to notice this. To our neighbor, the dour Mrs. Ridgley, and to my father and mother, John's target practice was just one more example of his confirmed juvenile delinquency.

When my father got home from work, Mrs. Ridgley was sitting on the porch swing, just swinging and waiting. She didn't want to talk to my mother. I walked in and out of the house several times—once to chase a ball, once to look for the cat—so I could hear what they were saying.

"Every single window on my sunporch," Mrs. Ridgley was saying, while my father nodded in silent rage.

"I know you've tried hard, but have you considered professional help?" she said a little later. I wondered what professional help meant. It sounded like the police. I began to feel a little sweaty, a little angry.

"I was going to report it, but if you'll make a substantial restitution perhaps I'll let it go this time," she went on. "But that boy shouldn't have guns."

I stopped in front of them on my way out of the house. I felt an unreasoning anger rise to my lips.

"Whatever it was, John didn't do it," I said. Why did I say that, I immediately wondered? Mrs. Ridgley flinched a little, as if she wanted to hit me but knew she had to restrain herself. My father looked furious.

"Why don't you run along and play in the park?" he said. So I did.

All these years later, it still seems surprising that I rose to my brother's defense. I don't know whether he was really verging on delinquency, but he had his moments. Once he leaned me out the third-floor window and threatened a longer trip for me if I ever touched his toy soldiers again. Another time he tricked me into letting him burn my lip with a magnifying glass. He regularly tripped me, pummelled me, spit in my general direction, and gave me pet names like "faggot" and "toilet face." And he had bigger problems, I knew: my mother had to go down to the police station to retrieve him a couple of times. Although he was never actually charged with a crime, everyone knew (or thought) that it was just a matter of time until John got caught with something too big to sidestep. Why, then, did I make a fool of myself and risk my father's wrath by speaking up for John?

In a cruel situation, rebellion is the obvious escape. It ought to lead to the freedom Philip Hallie describes. Where rebellion does not bring a clean break—and it often does not—the alternative is subversion. My brother and sister were rebels; I was subversive. They did bad things; I said peculiar things. I cannot believe I was conscious of this tendency when I was eight, or even when I was several years older. I wanted very much to love home and to feel secure there. If anyone had told me I was actually subverting a cruel home, I would have denied it to the hilt. But at some level my brother and sister and I all knew we were playing the same game. Why they were the active players, and I the passive one, I still do not understand. Perhaps the fact that there were two of them, barely twenty months apart, and only one of me had something to do with it. They had strength in numbers; they could mount uprisings. I was on my own.

But we faced a common enemy—not Mom and Dad exactly, or the physical surroundings they made for us, but a system of belief and a way of behaving that left us scared and hurt and dumbfounded. To be good children of the Father-Mother God, we had to fight all of our instincts. Worse yet, we had to watch our parents fight their instincts—their instincts to help us, to ease our pain, to let us be ordinary kids. And somehow we knew this meant death. Whatever we were, whoever we were, we could not be sawed and hammered to fit that beautiful mold of the perfect life. We fought back.

Or rather, John and Cin fought back; I watched, and waited. What I saw—as I watched, and listened, and read between the lines of the family tales—was a story that began, not with John and Cin, but with Mom and Dad, or perhaps with their own parents. My father's mother, I knew, had died of cancer when my father was a young teenager. From his father (my grandfather Harry) he had intuited an admonition to be strong, to keep his pain to himself. That's what he did. When World War II broke out a couple of years later, he signed up with the Navy, becoming one of their brightest pilots in a short space of time. Instead of sending him into combat, they made him a flight instructor at the Pensacola Naval Air Station in Florida. He was, by various accounts, a tough mentor and a good teacher. By the end of the war he had decided to leave the Navy and go back to college; he wanted to be a professor of engineering.

It didn't work out. After losing his temper with a calculus instructor at Drexel University, he quit school. A married man, he had a baby on the way. With thousands of vets looking for work, jobs were scarce. He went to work as a bookkeeper for a somewhat tyrannical uncle, then moved to the textile division of a large corporation. He was loyal, a good team player; he liked authority. If he had lost his chosen career in a fit of anger, he rarely discussed what might have been. He worked hard to make what actually happened more or less palatable. He traveled a great deal, leaving the kids to Mom. And from time to time he flew into a rage.

Where might he have gone if he hadn't done all the right things—hadn't married at the right time, hadn't had a baby at the right time, hadn't left the military at the right time? It's easy to speculate; he had everything going for him—a keen mind, an equally keen will, and exceptional mechanical skills. But he operated under drastic pressures. In the military he learned to defend a way of life which, from a sense of duty, he felt obliged to embrace during and after the war. And yet it seems that was not enough. Something made him self-destructive; there was something self-hating in him, something that seemed to track back to a mother who had vanished somewhat mysteriously without giving him a chance to say good-bye—or to understand. Home, which death had disrupted when he was a kid, caught up with him when he was an adult; he made it as perfect as possible, and he left often. Maybe not more often than other men of his generation—but often nevertheless.

He had an ideal companion in my mother, though as time went on they seemed deeply incompatible. They both liked authority and sought it out; they both liked someone or something to confirm that they were living a good life. Perhaps *liked* is the wrong word here; fundamentally I believe my mother detested authority, and would have fought it with an anarchist's zeal if she had seen any way out. But she didn't. The religion to which she swore allegiance was the gift of her stepfather, who entered her life when she was six. What had happened to her other father? No one ever mentioned him, and it was years before I found out even the smallest details of his life.

The stepfather, whom all the kids called Poppy, was earnest and faithful and demanding and kind. My mother adored him. He made his living selling insurance. In letters that came to me after my mother died—letters from Poppy to her, and from her to Poppy—I saw her efforts to please him by reporting all the good and virtuous events of her day, and his efforts to guide her toward divine goodness by precept and example. It was an ideal religious correspondence. Even before this, however, I knew that my mother thought Poppy was special—spiritually gifted in some way. It was Poppy who had convinced my grandmother to convert from the Southern Baptist faith to Christian Science. And it was Poppy who encouraged my grandmother to become, a bit later in her life, a Christian Science practitioner.

According to my mother, Poppy was also the man who refused to allow her to attend art school. He sent her instead to a good respectable women's college in Massachusetts. Poppy was the man who regularly warned my mother when she was a teenager that mortal mind offered many enticements, including the dissoluteness of art: a faithful daughter and churchgoer would recognize these enticements for what they were, and resist them.

My mother did not want to resist them. There was a wild side to her, a racy, daring will she barely kept in check throughout her youth. There was also the matter of talent. My mother was no dabbler. Her early paintings and drawings show exceptional ability, the kind an appraising parent would want to nurture. But Poppy, for all his kindness and dignity and passionate belief in the power of the spirit, was not a particularly appraising parent. Art was not a respectable profession; therefore my mother would not become an artist.

Nor would she marry an artist, or anyone remotely like an artist. Poppy had his stepdaughter's life in hand, and knew that she would marry a respectable and stable man—preferably someone with a distinguished military background, preferably someone the family had known for a while.

My father's family had come each summer to the same town in south Jersey for holidays; my mother's family also vacationed there. My mother and father grew into adolescence together on the beach, fighting and making up as if they sensed a deeper communion or antagonism. Their families became, if not friends, then warm acquaintances. Though my mother's family was slightly better off, the family fortunes and backgrounds were comparable. And, although my mother regularly told us that she hadn't liked my father and had had no intention of marrying him, the marriage took place. My mother devoted herself to the family and the church. Occasionally she painted.

From the canvases she left behind—a few finished, most unfinished—it seems clear that my mother had an odd, stark sympathy for the imperfect world within her and around her. The loneliness of a single tree in winter was more than mere style or contrivance; it was a projection of a feeling so intense that the tree became a shadow for my mother's consciousness. It was no wonder she could not finish that painting, since she could not really admit her feelings to herself. And yet the power of the painting was undeniable and comforting.

In her later work, she began to experiment with color as an alternative to form—painting her granddaughter Gwen, for example, in a field of California poppies, yet converting the field and the poppies to virtually pure color, defying their physical reality even as she carefully captured the physical reality of Gwen. There was still something suspect about the world in this painting, something that needed conversion into spirit. For my mother, color was—at least consciously—a metaphor for spirit. Yet the joy she took in mixing her paints, in savoring the difference between raw umber and burnt sienna, confirmed her desire to extend some kind of olive branch to the world. Her last work revealed a reciprocity between form and color, body and spirit, as if the isolated tree she had painted so many years before were no longer an emblem for loneliness, but for life.

And yet it all came to naught. I now believe that what my mother needed, particularly as a child, was the right kind of direction and encouragement. She needed the freedom to explore her own talent. What she got instead was kindness and cruelty. And the damage this caused was immense.

Her instincts told her to become an artist; her father and mother, who from her point of view were virtual transparencies for the Father-Mother God they celebrated, told her that her instincts were not to be trusted. Wanting to believe them, wanting to be loved, she turned from those instincts to the voice of authority: it became a sweet addiction for her. And there were plenty of authorities to go around.

The fundamental authority, of course, was the church, which separated good from evil and reality from unreality. It offered healing in exchange for obedience to its doctrine. Beyond that, however, was the matter of culture. My mother had two sons and a daughter. How should they behave? How should they look? For answers to these questions she turned to the early editions of Dr. Spock and to the women's magazines, which willingly told her the right time to feed and toilet train the kids, and the right way to dress them. These authorities also told her more: they told her that, in middle-class America, certain standards of dress and behavior were absolutely essential, and that any deviation from them suggested that the deviants were exactly that—ill-bred, negligible people.

But meeting or exceeding these standards required money, and my father did not make a particularly large salary. In comparison to my uncle Dick—an insurance executive in the tradition of his father (my mother's stepfather)—my own father was always stretched a little thin. I remember clearly our anxious family visits to my uncle's house, which had a "den" (how my mother wanted a den!) and carpeted stairs and a kitchen with a dishwasher. Though ultimately we acquired a dishwasher, and my mother arranged an upstairs room to resemble a study, the sense of inferiority remained. Uncle Dick also had a wife whose social skills were impeccable. The house was always enviably clean, the food was brilliant and showed the influence of the latest recipes, and the conversation always seemed stylish and smooth. Nothing could crush my mother as quickly as a visit to my uncle's house. The effects would last for days.

My mother understood that she failed the test of social acceptability. She was not a neat housekeeper, she was not a particularly talented cook, and—despite her deeply affectionate nature—she was not naturally gifted as a full-time mother. But her authorities made it clear that these talents were the essence of a meaningful life, and it was her unhappy task to spend forty years slipping and clawing at the hem of social approval.

I remember another side of her, which I almost never saw. When, a couple of years after I was born, we moved from a cramped little stucco house to a rambling, run-down brick house a few blocks away, we moved into the same neighborhood as an artist named Tom Bostelle. Bostelle was fairly well known in the area; his paintings sold well at local art shows, and he taught classes from time to time through the town arts center. He made his studio in the loft of a garage a couple of houses away from us.

I'm not sure how he and my mother met. She had known him at least since the spring of 1956, when he painted two family portraits—one of her, one of Cin. Did she realize, when she saw the new house, that she would be moving practically around the corner from his studio? I picture her out watering her roses in the garden as he was coming back from errands: perhaps they exchanged neighborly words.

Eventually she began to study with him, taking art classes when she could coax the money from my father. And once in a great while he would drop by during the day for a visit.

This, I knew even as a child, was a dangerous proposition because my father was a very jealous man. Even the slightest suspicion of another man in the background—even the most innocent contact—fired his rage. It was not beyond the realm of possibility for my father to show up in the middle of the day. There were times when he had to come home to pack for a sudden business trip, for example. For him to arrive and find Tom Bostelle, artist, having coffee in the kitchen with his wife would be a guarantee of big trouble, possibly bodily harm.

I remember eating lunch one day in our kitchen, with my mother taking things in and out of the refrigerator in her slow, exasperated way, when someone knocked on the back porch door. No one ever came to the back door. My mother went out to the screened porch, letting the door close behind her. I could not see what was going on, but I heard my mother's voice leap up.

"Oh, hello! Hi! I was just making lunch for Tom—I mean, you know, *my* Tom," (nervous laughter). "Won't you come in? I've just made some fresh lemonade." Scuffing footsteps. The porch door slamming shut.

"Well, I'd like some lemonade," Bostelle said, "but I also wanted to bring you this." He'd brought her a present: a Maurice Sendak lithograph, with a quotation from Isaac Bashevis Singer's *Zlateh the Goat and Other Stories*.

They came into the kitchen, where my mother showed it to me. She was ecstatic. I was unimpressed. It looked like a goat to me. Nevertheless I tried to be nice, because I was happy to see my mother look so happy. She seemed suddenly quite girlish, full of energy. And Bostelle was an interesting character. I liked to watch him, even though I didn't like him. He was always animated, and moved a little like Richard Burton. I knew him mostly as the man who yelled at me when I let my dog chase his cat.

Bostelle stayed only for a glass of lemonade and some quiet talk in the kitchen. My mother told me to go out and play as soon as I finished my lunch. I remembered his visit for years, though, because of the fresh air it brought to the house. The spell lingered for hours, or days: my mother seemed not only happy, but envigorated, the way people do when something deep and true in them is once again confirmed. Ultimately the mundane reality of her life drew her down again, but I was glad to have witnessed her brief resurrection at the hands of Tom Bostelle.

These events were rare. I mostly remember my mother as weary from her domestic duties. She was working against herself as a mother and a housewife, and all three of us kids knew it. To me she seemed sad; to my brother and sister she seemed false. They tested her constantly. As years dimmed the misery somewhat, she admitted that one of her favorite stories had to do with a particularly bad moment with Cin and John. Cin was three years old; John was two. Unable to stand their bad behavior any longer, my mother locked them—actually locked them—in the basement. A few minutes later she heard scraping noises, then the crash of breaking glass. As she ran to open the cellar door, she heard my sister say very clearly, "Don't worry, Johnny, I'll get you out." My sister had dragged some boxes over to a high window, climbed up, and broken it. Crawling through the broken glass, she dragged John free as well. By the time my mother caught up with them they were well down the block and still running.

My mother often told this story as an example of how unmanageable Cin and John were. But to me the striking themes of the story are how desperate my mother was with her motherhood and how early my sister and brother felt the need to escape. My mother could not cope; she imprisoned them. And they broke out of prison. These themes would emerge again and again. When my mother tried to turn Cin and John into mannerly society children—dressing them as elaborately as she could afford, insisting on refined eating habits at the dinner table, pushing them to make friends with the "nice" children at school—they dug in their heels. They shrieked at the nice clothes; they fought at the dinner table until my father had to send them to their rooms; they made friends with the "bad" kids at school, or didn't make friends at all. By the time they were heading toward their teens these patterns seemed ineradicable. I, who came into consciousness when my brother and sister were about ten and eleven, remember them simply as very smart, very mean, and very much in trouble. It got to the point where even if they weren't breaking rules, the grown-ups treated them as if they were— or were about to.

On rare occasions my parents went away for a weekend trip, and my grandmother—my mother's mother, whom we called Naner—would come up from her home in Florida to stay with us. Even though she was a Christian Science practitioner and spoke lovingly of the perfect identities of John and Cin, Naner was a little less sanguine about them at close range. Once, when I was about six, she came up to take care of us—it may have been for a week. I can picture her in the kitchen, trying to get dinner ready and talking quietly to herself. She always seemed a little confused in the kitchen. I think she was concentrating on dinner for me, because I was the most difficult child to feed. (I hated to eat—not out of any rebellious tendency, but because the thought of food often made me feel sick. Although I had been a large baby, and had eaten well until I was a little over two years old, I had become a significantly underweight child, anxious and irritable.)

While Naner was trying to decide what I might like, Cin came into the kitchen to help. Naner was planning to feed me some leftover tuna casserole, but Cin—pointing out that I didn't like fish—thought I might be happier with some equally leftover chicken. Suddenly they were arguing. My grandmother had a loud, hurt, whiny voice when she argued.

"Why, child," she said, "how dare you contradict me? I know what my baby needs! You're just a contrary child. Didn't your Mamma teach you manners?"

The speech went on, as it always did, with Cin trying in vain to cut in. I began to cry.

"I'm *not* contrary," Cin finally yelled. "I just wanted him to have something he likes for dinner, that's all." I ran out of the room, crying.

Behind me I heard my grandmother's whine turn into a vicious assault.

"Now look what you've done," she yelled back at my sister. "If you hadn't come in here, causing all this fuss, he wouldn't be crying now. He's the saddest boy on earth today, and I'm the saddest grandma."

Again she went on, but I didn't hear the rest because I was already under the covers of my bed, crying and covering my head with my pillow. I wanted my mother and father to come back—sort of; at least they would relieve us of this wild grandmother, who prayed and hugged and scolded as if the world were about to come to an end. But I remember knowing that I wanted something else, too—not Mom or Dad, not any other grownup, but just a way out, an escape. I wanted to be scooped up and carried away by an alien space ship or—well, anything—freedom—freedom, escape, and love were what I craved.

No aliens came for me. But something almost as astonishing happened. As I lay there, sniffling under my blankets, my sister came quietly into the room and crawled into bed with me. Holding me tightly, she cried and cried—the only time I had ever seen her cry.

"I'm sorry they hurt you," she said between the tears. "I'm sorry it's so bad here." I didn't say anything. I just hugged her back. And then, after a while, she got up and left.

Revelations like this were rare, but they were what ultimately bound me to my brother and sister. Something was wrong—our instincts told us so—but we couldn't reach out to anyone to confirm it. Or we couldn't for a while. As my sister got older, she withdrew more from my parents, fought with them more, began attending Friends Meeting against their wishes, and—shortly after high school—announced her plans to marry her high school music teacher. My father disowned her; her disobedience had been too much to endure. My brother's story was even more complicated. His rebellions took many forms—a rock 'n' roll band, adventures with the police, threats to drop out of school, refusals to go to college— but unlike my sister he faced the spectre of Vietnam. He did not fight; nor did he flee. He stood his ground, became a conscientious objector, and worked in a mental hospital and in a halfway house for several years. As maddening as this fate was, it led him away from my parents, who finally seemed bewildered at the way he had turned out. Their legacy of authority had been broken: the Father-Mother God who had guided my mother's parents, and my parents, seemed in some inexplicable way to lose hold of the next generation.

Of course it was not inexplicable at all. What *was* inexplicable—what remains difficult to fathom—was how my parents could have endured their own cruelty, and the cruelty inflicted upon them, for so long. When did they lose their desire for freedom—for independent thought, and a life in consonance with their most sustaining instincts? When did they decide that freedom was simply not an option?

In her diaries, which came to her children after she died, my mother writes, about a year before her death, of her escape plan. At some level she had never lost her desire for freedom. It stayed with her despite all that her parents did to rid her of it, and despite everything her church told her about her misconception of freedom. For over fifty years she had listened to the church tell her that she was free, and now—at age fifty eight—she had been a wife, mother, Sunday school superintendent, a reader in her church, a Christian Science reading room librarian, and an admired figure in her community. And yet, according to her diaries, she felt no less trapped than she did when she was eighteen.

She had been free to choose a life within a rigidly defined context; she had been free to make choices within a highly stable, highly structured universe. When she made those choices they brought her obligations—a husband, children, church duties—and because she was a profoundly loving and kind person, she took those obligations to heart for most of her life. In the end, however, she looked back to a more instinctual universe, an unstable realm where she could make choices not only within one context—the reality of Christian Science—but within several contexts. In fact she could choose her context; beyond the world her religion defined for her lay an open terrain. What she planned to do, then, was make *real* choices, choices which began to clarify her life. She would leave home and husband; she would travel; she would study the art she had so long neglected. She would become, finally, an artist.

As she was making these plans, in 1979, my mother noticed an odd swelling on her back. This was accompanied by wracking pains that awakened her in the middle of the night, and other symptoms that led her to believe she had cancer. Though she did not think that God was punishing her, she streaked back to her religion like a frightened fawn: she had to behave perfectly, she had to have perfect faith, or she would die. Ironically, there is some evidence to suggest that the kind of cancer she contracted has a very high rate of cure when treated medically. But she would have no doctors. In a way, it seems, this last illness was a test. She had declared her freedom; would her religion, would God, sustain her in her quest?

They would not.

2

THE ART OF TRAVEL

TRAVEL IS BY NATURE A SUBVERSIVE ACTIVITY. THIS IS TRUE, I think, even for the people in Hawaiian shirts and Reeboks who spend their days on Caravan buses, touring Vienna and Rome in air-conditioned splendor. When they return, they talk gladly about what an adventure it was, what a bunch of strangeness. They are glad to be home, where everything is the same. But everything is not the same: they have seen something they cannot evade. Either they will cling more forcefully to their xenophobia—which is itself a consequence of travel—or they will begin to wonder, slightly, if certain colors or sounds or fragrances from far away might not be as desirable as the ones back home. In resisting and in giving in to the lure of the new place, they subvert their old selves. They are not who they were.

For people who work harder to leave their old contexts behind, the change can be even more radical. This does not mean that travel equals epiphany. Not everyone leaves one day, like Gaugin, and winds up in Tahiti. But, absolved of the old contexts, one begins to fall back on the bare minimums of life: one's own identity, in whatever permutation it happens to take at the moment, and the randomness of stimuli which change it still further. Old patterns seem distant; voices from the past compete with new noises, the scraping sounds of the self getting up from its chair and looking out the window.

I was traveling—though I did not realize it—when I began to pull away from my parents and their religion, even as I kept myself firmly and faithfully in their tow. I saw no contradiction in this for many years. When I did, I begat a crisis. But the more I traveled, the more I began to see a way out. And this was true even though—ironically—I hated to travel. I still hate to travel: nothing is more uncomfortable, more compromising, more likely to induce a sense of cosmic abandonment. Also, despite my best efforts, I retain many of the neuroses of my childhood, which prevent me from eating comfortably in restaurants and from traveling comfortably in confined spaces, like airplanes. I am frequently a traveling basket case. And yet I still do it. In a way, it's the only game in town.

JERUSALEM. 6:00 A.M. SOME LONG JUNE DAY, PERHAPS THE FIRST official day of summer, 1984. An hour ago I left my friends' home in a suburb north of Tel Aviv to drive here. As I passed Emmaus on the road to Jerusalem, dawn crept once again over the center of the world. The sky was a wide, pale, shimmering rose, with fire behind it. Long streamers of sun struck the wreckage of homemade tanks and armored vehicles from the 1947–48 Israeli war of independence; they lay by the side of the road, blasted, overturned, coated in thick layers with red Rustoleum antirust paint. "Preserve, protect, defend," I said to myself, thinking of a presidential oath from another country halfway around the world. I myself have never fought in a war.

I pull into a gas station just outside the walls of the Old City of Jerusalem. The Arab attendant understands my request for a full tank and a quart of oil. I am driving my friends' antique Volkswagen bug, which came with them from the States when they were transferred to the embassy here. They have since bought a small but luxurious Peugeot station wagon, and have conferred the VW upon me for the duration of my stay in Israel. It's probably just as well that this VW and I have made an acquaintance. Brunhilde, as she is called, came to me virtually without oil, even though she'd been used regularly for commuting to the embassy. How she survived on a thimbleful of 10W-30 is beyond me. But I've been attending to her, and so far she's treated me very well.

This morning Brunhilde is taking my wife Lesley, my friend Jennie, and me to Masada. We plan to climb the Snake Path to the fortress, rather than take the aerial tram, and we hope to arrive before the desert heat overwhelms us. Lesley and Jennie are looking at the map, trying to guess the actual route out of Jerusalem. I am staring out the window, watching the new light turn the walls of the Old City golden.

Suddenly the attendant is at my elbow, gesturing, looking mournful. I follow him to the rear of the car, where he points a little bit to the right of the oil dipstick. What is it? It should be obvious to me; it certainly is obvious to him. When I finally see it, I'm astonished at my idiocy: how could I have missed it? There is nothing left of the fanbelt but a tough little thread of fabric. It's a miracle the car has come this far. Later I will find out that the fanbelt had never been replaced during the 180,000-mile life of the car, but right now I'm not in the mood to be impressed with longevity: what I've got is trouble. A broken fanbelt on an air-cooled VW in the desert is virtually instant disaster.

The attendant and I gesture at each other. I point to the thread of the belt, to the station, to him: does he have a new one? He looks disgusted, gesticulates at the service bay. Obviously he does not have a new one; the bay is empty. He sells gas and oil. Period. I bang my chest with my open palms and look distraught. How can I find a new one? He shrugs. He goes back to the office.

We drive the car around to the side of the gas station and consult, though there isn't much to be said.

"How far do you think we'd get?" asks Jennie.

"It must have been this way for awhile," says Lesley. "Isn't it worth the risk?"

No one says yes.

"Even if we could get a new fanbelt, no one here knows how to change it," says Jennie.

"I guess we'll have to get someone to tow it," says Lesley. "And we'll have to call Brady and Phyllis."

"In a couple of hours," Jennie says.

We nod. I go to the front, where the tool kit should be. There is no tool kit. There is no spare tire. There is no jack. All this mysteriously vanished when the car was shipped from the U.S. to Israel. Brady and Phyllis, fond owners of Brunhilde, managed to scrounge a lug wrench from somewhere, so that's here. There's also a big, rubber-handled screwdriver half hidden under the mat in the front compartment. So here we are—a car about to have its version of a coronary arrest, three adults with limited mechanical aptitude, a lug wrench, and a screwdriver. And the sun continues to rise over this confluence of the world's religions and cultures, where in a time-honored tradition we are suddenly at a loss for what to do.

The heat comes early with the sun, and after focusing for a few minutes on our strange situation I begin to drift. Volkswagens have hummed and shuddered in and out of my life since I was eight; I remember going to school in them, going to the shore in them, having accidents in them, and, later on, making love in them. The engines always have that funny, throaty-smooth sound, as if something is not quite in balance; I would hear that sound often on autumn afternoons when, among the fallen leaves, I would watch my father tune the engine out in front of our Pennsylvania house. He'd show me where to push on the carburetor to make the engine rev. He'd tell me about the intake and exhaust valves, and he'd show me how the timing light caught the flywheel either at top dead center or slightly off. Sometimes he'd loosen the big nut on the alternator—the same size as the lug nuts on the wheels—and let me hold the little washers that made the fan belt looser or tighter.

Now my mind goes blank for a second, the way it always does when I'm about to have some useful idea. It's true I'm not a mechanic, but I did watch my father work on the car when I was a kid, and I *did* watch him change a fanbelt—I can almost see it again, I can see him holding the new belt in his hands, see it squirming like a young snake.

"I can fix this."

"What?"

"We don't need a garage," I say. "We only need a place that sells parts. I can fix this. I used to watch my dad do it. All you need to change a VW fan belt is a lug wrench and a screwdriver."

It's true; as my father used to say admiringly, it is an astoundingly simple design. You don't even really need the screwdriver, just a metal shim or even a doubled-over coathanger to stick into the hole in the alternator and lock the system. Of course this didn't necessarily help us; it meant that we didn't need to leave the car in garage *if* we could find a parts store somewhere in Jerusalem. But with all the VW's around, that seemed likely; and it seemed equally likely that our thread of a fan belt would at least allow us to prowl around the city.

Since it was only 7:00 A.M. at this point, we drove toward the center of the new city, where we knew the luxury hotel crowd would just be cranking up. In one of the hotels we found a desk clerk who thought he remembered a parts store not too far from the American Colony Hotel in east Jerusalem. After getting lost several times, we found the place—an old quonset hut with a platoon of wounded VWs scattered around a fenced-in yard. The shop was not scheduled to open for at least a half-hour, so Lesley and I went over to use the bathrooms at the American Colony Hotel while Jennie took care of the car. By the time we returned, mechanics and customers were hanging around the shop drinking coffee, and Jennie was standing by the car with the fan belt she had already bought. I installed the new belt at the curbside in a few minutes. We made it to Masada with no trouble.

But all along the way, as we came down into the Jordan River valley and drove beside the Dead Sea, I kept thinking about my father. For the past several years he had hardly been a part of my life at all; even before then, he had often been a distant presence, traveling or working late or holing up in his electronics workshop to build the latest Heathkit. Did I like him? That wasn't the right question. I had been trying for years to get away from him, even though we never saw much of each other. His authoritarian self loomed in my mind like a gate at a railroad crossing, always threatening to descend.

Unlike my brother and sister, I had never fought him, but I had fought what he represented. From high school on, I built my life to swerve away from his. I rejected science and engineering for art and literature; I wrote poetry; I won literary awards that made him equally proud and confused. And he—to his credit—let me go; he rarely lowered his railroad gate on me, as he had on John and Cin. He never urged me to attend any specific college, as he had with them, and he never threatened me with a funding cutoff or disownment because of what I was studying. Perhaps John and Cin had worn him out, or perhaps my method—subversion, not rebellion—simply worked better: I did what I did quietly, unobtrusively, and very stubbornly.

Yet, after all our distance, my father made a cameo appearance as a lifesaver. I learned something important from him, and it came in handy not in West Chester, Pennsylvania, or in Palo Alto, California, but in Jerusalem, a city he would not really have approved of. I took up traveling, quite reluctantly, seven years before this particular trip, because I could no longer survive the silence and sadness of home; I had to get away. In traveling, at least, I thought I would break those bonds. It didn't work quite that way.

I made the God of my childhood loosen his grasp on me, and to that extent my mother and father went away as well. But from time to time, they reappeared—not as harmful and wounded people, but as interesting people with hidden lives, lives that were somehow incommensurate with their roles. My subversions had not fully brought me freedom, but they brought me occasional glimpses of people I had lived with but had not known, people momentarily isolated from the cruelties of their lives.

My FATHER, WHO SUFFERED FROM SO MANY PRIVATE GRIEFS, WAS not an easy man to get along with, but in one respect he was magnificent: he was unfailing in his devotion to machines of almost any variety. When he chose to, he could talk to me at length on the virtues of, say, the 1966 Chevrolet four-barrel carburetor, or the drawbacks of the Wankel rotary engine. Talking, however, was not his strongest suit; he was a man of action. As he liked to point out, talking would never make an engine run more smoothly.

On weekends sometimes, or on his rare summer days of vacation, he would encourage me in my first and last steps toward automotive literacy. He would allow me to stand beside him as he worked on the car, and when he needed a simple tool—a crescent wrench or needlenose pliers—I would be allowed to hand it to him. And when I was twelve, he and my daring mother bought me a motorcycle.

It was a 50-cc Benelli motocross bike—neither new, nor large, nor powerful, nor expensive. But it gave form and life to my imaginings. No longer did I have to confine myself wistfully to magazine photos of high-speed turns and hair-raising rides through rough country. I had the thing itself—

the device that would make these experiences possible, at least to some degree.

And, although I did not know it at the time, I also had a new kind of lexicon. The motorcycle was a compendium of gears and springs and sprockets and cylinder heads and piston rings, which between my father and me acquired the force of more affectionate words that we could never seem to use in each other's presence.

Almost immediately the Benelli became a meeting ground, a magnet for the two of us. We would come down to look at it—even if it was too late in the day for a good ride—and my father would check the tension of the chain, or examine the spark plug for carbon, or simply bounce the shock absorbers a few times as he talked. He'd tell me about compression ratios and ways of downshifting smoothly into a turn; I'd tell him about my latest ride, when I leaped two small hummocks or took a spill on a tight curve.

More rarely, he'd tell the stories of his youth. His favorite, which he recounted in slightly different versions about four times a year, had to do with the go kart he built in his father's house during the Depression. It was by any account a masterful performance. He managed to pick up a small, broken gasoline engine for free, and tinkered with it until it came back to life. The wheels, steering gear, axles, chassis—all were scrounged for a few cents, or for free, from junkyards and vacant lots in and around Philadelphia.

Winter was in full swing when my father had his go kart ready for a test drive; snow lay thick on the ground. He'd built the kart in his father's large basement, and given the weather he felt it made sense to make the trial run indoors. His engineering skills were top-notch. Assembled from orphaned parts, the go kart performed like a well-tuned race car. My father did what any good thirteen-year-old would have done: he got carried away. He laid on the power coming around the corner of the basement, lost control, and smashed head-on into the furnace. It was a great loss for him. The jagged wood and metal cut and bruised him; he had destroyed his brand-new car. Far worse was the damage to the furnace. In 1933 such damage was almost more than the family finances could sustain. Furious, my father's father called him names, upbraided him for his stupidity and irresponsibility, and made him feel worthless. Years later, as he would tell this story to me, my father would linger over those words—"stupid," "irresponsible"—as if the pain had never gone away.

In these moments he and I had a common stake in something. Though he might not know whether I was reading at the eighth-grade level or the twelfth-grade level, or whether my math scores lagged behind those of the rest of the class, he was delighted to see that I knew how to adjust a clutch cable or stop after a low-speed, controlled skid. These skills were a source of genuine adventure for me, and I came to life when he observed my progress.

But this was only part of our rapport with the motorcycle. My father found few occasions to be overtly tender with the family, but he could be tender with a machine. I began to notice this in the countless small adjustments he regularly made. His touch on the cranky carburetor settings for gas and air was gentle, even soothing; at least it seemed to sooth the motorcycle, which ran smoothly under his touch but not under mine.

I found that, from time to time, this tenderness buoyed me up in its wake. If my father was, in his dreams, a flat-track mechanic, then I was his driver: he owed me the best he could give me; that was his job. This dream of his bound us in a metaphor which, at its heart, was not so different from the kind of straightforward love another child might have received from a more accessible father. I did not know this then, not exactly. But I knew, when we both hovered over the Benelli's cylinder head or gearbox, adjusting a valve or replacing a gasket, that he would not have worked on this machine for himself alone.

Yet there was a secret to our new language, a secret that only slowly revealed itself. What we shared through the motorcycle contradicted most of our other encounters in the family. It was almost as if we lived in another world when we came together over this machine, and for a time I hoped that this world might be the new one, the ideal on the horizon. I was wrong. The bands of our words were strong, but too narrow to encompass the worlds rising before me.

Almost without knowing it I began to acquire other vocabularies—the tough, subtle speech of girls, the staccato syllables of independence, the wrenching words of love and emptiness. In this I began to leave my father behind. He could not talk of these things with me. He remained with his engines; and long after I had ceased to ride it, he would occasionally open the gas jets, prime the carburetor, and take my motorcycle for a spin around the block.

But as it seems that nothing is ever wholly lost, this vocabulary of the garage and the flat-track speedway still has a kind of potency, a place in the scheme of things. When I had dinner recently with my father after not having seen him for nearly a year, we greeted each other with the awkwardness of child cousins: we hardly knew what to say. I had almost given up on the possibility of a prolonged conversation until I happened to mention that my car needed a new clutch. Suddenly we were safe again, as we moved from the clutch to the valves on his souped-up VW and the four-barrel carburetor on the '66 Chevrolet Malibu, still pouring on the power after all these years. We had moved back to the language of our old country. And though one of us had journeyed far and had almost forgotten the idioms, the rusty speech still held, for a time, the words of love.

"THE WORDS OF LOVE." IN *HOLY THE FIRM*, ANNIE DILLARD recalls that the seraphim worship God in perfect love, while the cherubim, the next lower order of angels, worship Him in perfect knowledge. "Love is greater than knowledge," Dillard writes. "How could I have forgotten?" But love is not enough. Love is not the sole healing force in the world. Love may even reinforce cruelty, as it did in my family, rather than eradicate it. Perhaps the problem lies with the idea of seraphim, for what is perfect love? What do we know of it? Our loves are various and partial. Saint John said, "Perfect love casteth out fear," but who among us is not afraid? We are creatures of knowledge as well as love. Sometimes knowledge is the only antidote to imperfect love.

For some time now I've wondered about the form my subversions took within the family and the religion. The pairing of love and knowledge, I think, must have had something to do with it. This was not a harmonious pairing; it was a mis-yoking, in which the team could not pull straight, and finally could not pull at all. I loved my mother and father. I was grateful to them for protecting me, and for sheltering me from the dangerous world. I was grateful to God, in whatever way I conceived of Him, for filling my life with words and ideas: He was the forcefield who protected me from my own mortal body, and from the death-filled meanings of ordinary human life. There was nothing calculated or rational about this love. It was an immutable fact, a given, as real as my own existence.

I *knew* other things. What did I know? It will take some time to sort it all out. By the time I was a teenager, however, it was clear that I had begun to discover a whole other world, a third world, to compete with the sheltering world of my parents and the spiritual world of my church. This was a world of risk and adventure, solace and beauty. It took shape around me until it became a state of mind. I knew that I could go, and "learn by going where I have to go," as Theodore Roethke said. In this other world, my life seemed less defined, less certain, more rich in possibility; the voices that clamored for me to behave or think in a certain way grew more faint.

In California, where my parents and I moved when I was thirteen, the coastal range rose up in succeeding ridges and valleys only a few miles west of our house. It was possible to reach the Pacific within an hour. It was also possible to

spend hours, or even days, lost in the wide wilderness of these
last of the continent's mountains. At first I would bicycle into
the range. Later, when I had my license, I would vanish for
whole days onto the back roads and footpaths of the redwood
forests. As a photographer for the yearbook in high school,
I had what was then regarded as a perfectly natural excuse
for cutting classes. The yearbook needed pictures, and I was
obliged to provide them. How this excuse held water I do
not know: my high school was well known for its academic
rigor. It may have been that everyone there simply trusted
me. For whatever reason, I was occasionally permitted to
leave the school grounds by about 10:00 A.M. and not return
until the next day.

Although the coastal range begins only a few miles south
of San Francisco, it remains largely wild and undeveloped.
An hour's drive swung me down Old La Honda Road, past
isolated houses and abandoned farms, to the small town of
La Honda, crumbling into the redwood dust of the forest.
Bikers on Harleys would stop there for sandwiches and
drinks. Heading east on Highway 84, I would come back to
Skyline Drive and cruise south to Alpine Road. A right turn
there, past the pond and the tall golden ridges, would send
me toward the heart of the redwood forests and Pescadero.

I was not only free on those roads, I was safe—safer than
I had ever been before. It was a primal world where I spent
equal time doing and observing. People came and went with
great ease in cars and on motorcycles, and when they vanished
they were gone. No deposit, no return. It seemed to be a
classic world without obligations (although later I would learn
how wrong this view could be). More important, it was a
world of impulse and intuition: you did what you wanted to
because it seemed right at the time. This was new to me. It
was safe because no tricks were being played. The world here
was not a dangerous illusion, and death was not a terrifying
or devilish unreality. The land here was very beautiful, and
you could get lost in it. It was an open universe. You could
travel through it. You could leave your old games behind.

On impulse I would hike to the old Page Mill; on impulse I would hike back out and drive to the sea. Digging my feet into the sand, turning my back to the piles of driftwood left by a recent storm, I would sit until my glasses clouded up with salt spray. Then I would drive north, towards Half Moon Bay, where pumpkins were ripening in the fields and mothers with children were coming in from San Bruno or San Carlos or Belmont to buy their Halloween centerpieces. I watched them all; I drove on.

Who was I there? Again the wrong question. I remember feeling a certain quietness, a separate peace. It seemed more important to know who I wasn't. I wasn't the frightened child, waiting for the world to strike me with its latest evil. I wasn't the excessive scholar, doing hours of homework each night to prove my right to exist. I wasn't the dutiful son, staying close to his family and his Father-Mother God. With each mile I drove I left some part of each of these identities behind, until by the end of the day I felt simply lighter. I was less, somehow, than I had been before. I was almost nothing. This put me on the same level of being with everything I saw—the sand, the waves, the sequoias, the crumbling buildings of the tiny roadside towns. And that was not bad. That was knowledge. That was good. I was discovering, for the first time, that I could be on intuitive terms with the physical world—a world that, according to my religion, did not actually exist.

But, like a tide, this discovery rose and fell depending on my identity at the moment. For the first time I began to see that my identity, my self, could be in severe flux. The person I knew to be myself, the lighter soul on the road, could slip fluidly back to being the person I had always accepted as myself—the good boy, the devoted servant of the Lord. And there were gradations, shades of selfhood: when I went to Fort Funston or Pescadero Beach with kids from Sunday school, who was I then? I was all of these people. I was a cacophony of voices, I was a tumult of sincerities and made-up faces, I was a series of clever inventions.

In the midst of pure being, it does not matter who you are. That may be life's greatest blessing. But that kind of nurturing absence, that perfect knowledge, descends rarely. The rest of the time one exists with imperfect knowledge and imperfect love, trying to put on a good show. I was putting on a virtual three-ring circus, and at some point I could not hold it together. What I loved, or had learned to love, would not sustain me, just as it had not sustained my mother. More than one slate of the soul had to be wiped clean. At some point, because my love was not perfect, I had to trust in knowledge to direct my escape. But this was almost impossible. It was also terrifying.

BACK IN REAL TIME, AS THE COMPUTER ADDICTS SAY, I LIVE JUST outside Boston, in a house with three flats, known locally as a triple-decker. The houses are close together; through the half-open curtains I can see our neighbors' kitchen window, opaque in the midday sunlight. These neighbors have lived here for forty years, raising their children and watching land values skyrocket. Now they are sitting on a gold mine, while a new generation of parents moves in with too few children and too little money.

It's restful, sometimes, to think the thoughts of an adult: half my income for rent, another quarter for daycare—what will we use to buy groceries or fix the car? Nothing is more aggravating than the illusion of money, but nothing is more ubiquitous. Everyone I know has run a credit card out to the limit, everyone is hoping the economy hangs on just a little longer, everyone is coaxing nine-year-old cars to the garage for $900 repairs. These are the habits, the parameters, of our lives. They make us angry; they give us stability.

I come back to this now, of course, because it's a stability with a bite to it: we pay dearly for buying into the system. These same thoughts, when they are not comforting me, leave me with the sordid feeling of emptiness that started this whole project. How did I get to this point? What have I done that I can call my life?

Given the choice of habit or the terror of change, I might well choose habit. "Myself must I remake," the poet William Butler Yeats said, but he was more sanguine than I. Discarding the old self, or selves, is like giving in to death, or traveling too far. We can never come back. Voices echo down the corridors of loneliness. Terror is the dividing line, the river Styx. Stay on this side, the old self says: keep me, and I will keep you.

Yet circumstances sometimes run full-force against the old self, and what is left is a wound—an emptiness that is not quite empty, not full of peace or perfect knowledge. This is the home of fear. The old identity collapses like a great sky-scraper pancaking flat onto the ground, the tremors echoing all through the body. It's no wonder they call it a nervous breakdown, when nothing the body and the mind can tell each other seems to work. All the pieces are still there, but something's missing—some formal principle, some way of making sense of the cataclysm.

Darkness, pain, anxiety, shivering, sweat, nausea, despair—this is the emptiness when the old self collapses. It is not the familiar emptiness of the middle class, nor is it the lightness I knew in my early travels on the road.

What is it like? It is like this: you are on a night flight, and you are so sick you cannot rise from your seat except to retch. You have forgotten your destination; everyone around you is a stranger. They do not know what to do to help. They do not want to help, because in your illness you are alien to them; you are a threat to their happy and adventurous selves. The engines drone on. Beyond the small, scratched window, the world is dark. You will never land. That is what it is like.

These memories are very painful; even now, years later, they drag me toward a vortex where I cannot breathe. What keeps me going is the territory just beyond terror and despair, where the airplane, which is not supposed to arrive, does

arrive. I blink, look out at the colors of the world, and shiver.
The inward and the outward traveling have come to the same
thing, a new beginning. What could be more grim? Love,
the imperfect love of the old things, has failed. Knowledge
is austere, overwhelming. How do I begin to rebuild, after
my private Dresden? Nothing but an act of will will do. I
take small breaths—deep ones bring more nausea—and begin
to search the new terrain for clues.

ENGLAND. IT IS 1977, AND I AM TWENTY-ONE. I AM WALKING
in a wood that seems to have no end. The path, formerly
wide enough for a small car or truck, has dwindled to a horse
path and then to something less. No one has been this way
in many weeks. The first autumn leaves, falling a bit early
for whatever reason, lie unmoved on the path. The slow
weight of life here seems to be pulling things toward the
ground. Tired, I sit beside a tree and wait. Nothing happens.
A few leaves fall, making no sound.

Some distance behind me—whichever way that is—is
Cliveden House, the former estate of the second Viscount
Astor and his more famous wife Nancy. I am in Great Britain,
and I have no sense of home. I live among strangers, who
also happen to be my fellow college students. Cliveden House
is an overseas campus for Stanford University, and along with
sixty or so other people I am studying Anglo-American law.
But that is not really what I am doing. Mostly, each day, I
am talking to myself in the early hours of the dawn, trying
to convince myself to get out of bed.

This is a bad time. I do not want to think about it. I will
look at the trees. They are very quiet. There is no wind.
Making up an arbitrary sequence, I look from tree to tree,
trying to notice variations in the striated bark. There is no
point; I get tired easily these days, from all my waking and
walking. Better just to sit, now, and not think.

That is the problem: how do you not think? When you are damned, as I am, it is hard not to wonder about your condition. It is hard not to run screaming through the woods. It requires an act of will just to sit.

Willing myself to sit, I try to will myself not to think—a last-ditch approach. It never works. In fact my pattern of thought is depressingly familiar. Comfort comes first: I remind myself that, in my religion, God is love. This truth is unwavering. It does not waver despite all the pain I endured as a child; it does not waver despite the pain my parents inflicted on their children and on each other. God's love does not waver even if it has no effect. I sigh. *That* is certainly a comfort.

But it gets worse. There is, I know, a catch to God's love in my religion. I understand why it is there. If we were all simply taught that God is love, then anyone could do anything and claim that the goodness or badness of his deed did not matter. God loves the good and the bad; why, then, make any effort to be good? This thought frightens us. We are always trying to work out ways to get around it. In my case, I learned that although God is love, and is constantly giving His love to His creatures, they can choose to place themselves outside God's love by behaving badly. They can refuse God's love by their actions even if they embrace it in their hearts.

There are Christian Scientists who have placed themselves beyond God's care by believing in the reality of the mortal world, for example. I know about some of these people; a few have been my acquaintances, my companions in church. They are the Christian Scientists who suddenly disappear from Sunday school. Rumors streak among the students about sex, drugs, or medical operations. Such people have become different from us; they have fallen prey to the other reality, which we know to be unreal. We are still safe, because we still believe in the essential spirituality of the world. We do not seek sex; we do not try drugs; we do not take medicine; we do not go to doctors. We are good, that is, spiritually pure, and therefore we are free to receive the love of God.

Freedom again. I lean back hard against the tree, banging my head on the rough bark. It feels good. It feels real. The idea of freedom has weighed me down for months now. I have no freedom. I have no future. My life in unreal. I am beyond God's love.

Of course I am not damned. Christian Science acknowledges no hell. But there is something worse. There is life in the mortal world—utterly random, without authentic cause and effect, liable to every evil and disease and mutation known to the depraved mortal mind. I am in that world now. I cannot speak of hell, but I can speak of my current condemnation, for which I alone am responsible. It is a hell to me.

A slight wind jars the branches; perhaps it is only a crow taking off. It seems out of place here, in this vaguely hypnotic place. A leaf falls on my knee. If I stay here long enough, leaves will cover me completely.

Four years ago, in California, I fell in love with a woman whose touch wound hot threads of reality around my body like an electrical charge. I fell in love with her taste, her glance, the touch of her hands, her whole being, so that sex—which had before seemed something strange and distant, like a book with a blurred cover on a shelf—now seemed necessary and generous, a kind of completion. It was a new kind of knowledge—a knowing love, a combined physical and psychic power I had never known before.

Looking back, I am surprised at how long it took my sense of condemnation to gather like a great dark thundercloud. A year went by; two years. My lover and I quarrelled, saw our different futures, and broke up. Then came the low voices of doom. Through love I had entered the mortal world, and it was beautiful. It was also dangerous. And I had chosen it over God's real world without really thinking. Now, fully alert to the pleasures of the body, I could not get back. God's love moved serenely through a spiritual world I had once inhabited, but that was not my world. Everything I had learned about Him in Sunday school, everything I had ever been told, confirmed for me that I had engaged in the primal sin, and that by this error I had moved away: He would not call me back, for that was not His task.

Slowly, then remarkably fast, I began to come apart. The fact that dreadful things did happen in the world was further proof than anything could happen—homicide, infanticide, chemical warfare, insoluble webs of lies and hatreds, a Boschian scenario of insane horrors. By the spring of 1977, I lay in bed all night without sleeping. During the day, I could not eat. I could not go outside. In public places I would break into a sweat, fight nausea, begin to shake. I shook constantly; the world was a dark monolith which could not know me. I could not sit in classrooms, nor could I concentrate on my work. Dropping out of college, I went to live in Los Altos with my parents, who could not help me. They sent me to practitioners who determined that nothing was wrong with me, and that I had only to recognize God's love to be healed. I went home and threw up.

When you believe yourself to have left a closed universe, and everyone around you still lives in it, you have nothing to say and no source of comfort. I had no rest. What I did have, however, was an act of fate which I had placed in motion months before without realizing it. Virtually on a whim, I had filed an application with the Stanford Overseas Studies Office to study for a summer in England. After a few months went by, they notified me that I was well down on the waiting list; I would be wise to plan something else for my summer. In mid-May, however, I received a different message. A number of people had dropped out of the program; the waiting list had shifted dramatically. Did I want to go?

I looked at the letter, then looked at myself in the mirror. I was very sick. I had lost a good deal of weight, I trembled almost constantly. If Stanford knew my condition, I realized, they would not let me go. I walked around the house. No one else was home. It was quiet and dark, as it always was, like a tomb. As full of terrors as I was, staying would lead to death. I had to go.

So I am here, in England, aware that I am hanging on to sanity with slim determination. I look down at my hand. A mouse is sitting there. He is sitting beside my left hand. I can see his small flanks move in and out quickly as he breathes. He is staring up at me. His whiskers twitch, his nose quivers. His eyes are darker than anything I have ever seen. I stare back. Still he does not move. His eyes are so dark that I seem to be able to see right through them, to enter them and pass into a dark tunnel where, right in the center, unchanging, unreceding, stands a pinpoint of light. I am gliding down the dark corridors of his eyes toward a light that never shifts, that is precisely around me. I do not glow. I am dark. It is very restful here. Here seems to last for a long time.

When I come back out, the mouse has turned away. He is foraging; then, suddenly, he darts under a blanket of leaves and disappears. I see a rustling as he departs. Words come into my head.

"There is a real world. You can get to it. You cannot believe in it. It is not a matter of faith. When you are there, your life is whole. When you are elsewhere, even in the realm of faith, your life is not whole. You must prepare to travel to find this world. It is usually one step from where you are. Above all, you must be prepared to *look*."

My head hurts as if struck physically with this heresy. Who is preaching to me this way? It is my voice saying these things. I seem to have stepped under a waterfall. I am drenched. Can this be sweat, all over my body, all through my clothes? Though I am not at peace, the bad thoughts have been drowned out for a moment. I feel as if I have been shocked somehow, and though I know the bad thoughts are still there I cannot feel them or hear them. Something else, more than I can take in, has intervened. I left home to come here; now— here—where have I gone? I look around. Nowhere is the answer. Sighing, I stand up. I am soaked to the skin, and tired. There is nowhere to go but back to the house. The walk will be a long one.

ABOUT AN HOUR SOUTH OF BOSTON, A FEW MILES NORTH OF the place where God-riddled pilgrims anchored the May-flower, the Duxbury beach runs for several miles along an edge of cool blue sea. It is the weekend after Labor Day. No one is here. The food stand and beach shop are boarded up; sand laps against the sides of the buildings. It could be mid-November, or even February, for all the beach crowd cares; they have gone elsewhere. But it is still warm here, and the afternoon light angles down onto the sand in a golden genuflection.

My son Nathaniel and I are building a sand castle. The sand here is excellent for building, fine-grained and stable under compression. While Nathaniel digs holes and pats the sand into round towers, I start on a wall that will take me half an hour to complete. It will be the Great Wall of Duxbury, impregnable except by ocean or errant joggers. Piling the sand high, I pat it down and smooth it as if I were shaping clay on a potter's wheel. The sand is sensuous and obliging.

Long years of travel have brought me to this rich, empty beach. I think about this, a little idly, as I build, because building sand castles is a way of making idle thoughts count. It has been many years since I have felt comfortable enough to build a castle. Nathaniel clearly encourages my old engi-neering instincts. He is also one of my longest travels, another journey just beginning.

After a while in the sand, building and shaping my great wall, I take a break to rest my back and look around. Where am I? Since I've never been to this beach before I can't quite place myself for a moment. I could be anywhere; I could be halfway around the world, south of Haifa or just east of the Camargue. Does it matter? I feel a rush of freedom.

Why? Why? I crave this; where did it come from so suddenly? My mind zips back to the woods of Cliveden, to the
mouse and that brink of disaster: that was a rush of freedom
as well, so sharp and fast that I could not grasp it. Obviously
I have not grasped it yet. But why there, and then again here?
Is there a connection?

I was a newcomer there. I'm a newcomer here as well,
having moved from California barely a month ago. My rou-
tines, all my ways of doing things, are disrupted. All I can
think about is how much I'd rather be in San Francisco. I'm
a model of homesickness. Yet here, in the midst of this unknown place, I get a dose of something that really matters. I
have no familiar context, therefore I am free.

I wonder, is reality always an escape from context? Or do
we crave the real, the authentic experience, so much that we
create private contexts right out of our souls—arbitrary
breaths of fresh air that nurture us? Did the mouse come to
me like Gabriel, or did I invent his meaning in a moment of
utter despair? Did my father surround himself with machines
to escape the world, or to make it more real?

Most of the time these kinds of questions remain opaque,
but now I see how they start to answer themselves. We are
constantly creating reality out of our own needs. The real
does not exist apart from us, and it is not handed to us like
a great puzzle from the Newtonian God of Solvable Myster-
ies. We spin it out of ourselves like a great web, digesting
even those subatomic and unseeable events which run beyond
us like the wide range of air. Yet we also consent to give up
our reality making for the sake of . . . emptiness, adulthood.
After a while, what becomes important is not the act of con-
structing many mansions for the soul. What becomes important is the act of reducing those mansions to market value.
How much can we get per square foot? Will the client like
our report? Is the raise enough to cover a second mortgage?
Does the project extend a respected tradition? Does the book
reflect the influences of Fichte? Nietzsche? Hemingway? We

play in other people's realities after they are long dead, and after they have lost all control over the initial visions they set in motion. We play in the sandbox of dead and unreal women and men.

My father played in that sandbox, but he had his refuges too. And sometimes, while he adjusted a valve or replaced a gasket, I touched the border of his fragile sanctuary. Otherwise, between us, there was an unbridgeable gulf of unreality—actions without meanings, dead rituals, beliefs when no belief was required, rules when no rules could help. And now I play with my son, not in a sandbox, but on the random sand of the wide world, where a castle is as real as anything else.

Nathaniel is running down the beach now, laughing to himself and chasing the gulls. For very good reasons, he has grown tired of his dull father, who stopped building a perfectly good wall to sit in the sand and think. I run after him. The blood pounds in my head; surf splits around me as I try the waves. Soon I can hear nothing but the waves and the wind and the sound of my son laughing before me as I catch up to him.

3

RIDING AGAIN

I'M RIDING AGAIN. I'M ON MY WAY ACROSS THE COASTAL mountains of Northern California to the high bluffs overlooking the Pacific. The road switchbacks wickedly, and my motorcycle revs with no complaints as I downshift into a left hairpin. Aiming for the cliff ahead, I slide my gaze up to the left and countersteer. The bike leans over hard: I feel the deadly softness of gravel under my rear tire, but I don't skid. I'm through the turn. In the half-second I have to prepare for the next one, I shift to the left side of the lane, ready to lean into the ground if the curve is tight.

I've ridden motorcycles since I was twelve, and I'm glad to be out here today. This road is always a challenge, demanding that I draw on all the skill I've acquired over the last twenty or so years. But these days there's a difference to my riding. The difference is a small voice in the back of my head. It kicks in every now and then when I'm stopped at a light or accelerating out of a turn or passing someone on a straightaway. "Nathaniel," the voice says.

Nathaniel is eleven months old. Almost every father thinks his kid is gorgeous, and I'm no exception. Nathaniel's blond hair is like spun gold, and he's interested in everything. Even the most ordinary objects, such as light poles or the plastic covers on my high school yearbooks, make him point and exclaim. When he wakes from a nap and I go in to rescue him from the confines of the crib, he stands reaching for me. He has one goal in mind—to get me to pick him up, to liberate him. I'd never want to lose him. Nor would I want him to lose me.

And yet here I am, riding a small rocket on a road where serious motorcycle accidents average one or two a week. Isn't this a kind of lunacy? I must be shirking my responsibilities as a father. "You're not still *riding,* are you?" a friend asks. "How can you—you know, with a kid and all?"

It's the "and all" that always gets me. A child is never simply a child, but a creature with severe consequences for fathers. The baby arrives and—bang—the man emerges from his stag-room chrysalis into winged fatherhood: he becomes a beautiful specimen of caution, foresight, and self-sacrifice.

There are, I know, men who can sacrifice the essential pleasures of life in the hope that their sacrifice will somehow benefit their children, but I find that I cannot live this way. In fact, I have serious doubts that such sacrifices work. No amount of money can guarantee my son's happiness or stability. No amount of caution on my part will protect me from, say, the one driver who happens to run a signal when I am crossing. Despite my ardent desire not to lose my son, I will lose him someday, and he will lose me. This will happen as surely as I lost my mother—and my uncle Sandy, dead when he was five years older than I am now.

No one could have been more transformed by parenthood than Sandy. Although I was still a kid, I remember when he stopped leaping off high—really high—sand dunes. I recall the way he put his fondness for sports cars into the closet with his models. Ultimately he seemed to give up most of what I remember as being unique and lively about him. He devoted himself to his insurance business. He bought a nice suburban ranch home where his kids could play in the yard and even run into the street without much fear of danger. When he died suddenly of kidney failure at the age of thirty-six, no one could believe it. His life, and his family's life, had seemed so secure.

I think of Sandy sometimes on the days when I'm taking care of my son. Nathaniel's walking now, and when we take a stroll outside, he regularly leads me to the motorcycle. Though he's much too young to be a passenger, he's happy to have hands-on experience in the carport. He likes to whack the long chrome exhaust pipes, and when he touches the wide rear racing tire he pulls his hand away fast and giggles, as he does when he's touched something hot. Sitting on the seat bores him—it's too far away from anything interesting—but when he's wearing his soft leather moccasins, I let him crouch down on the gas tank. From there he can reach up to tap the speedometer and the tachometer with their bright clear numbers and red-tipped needles. Inside, he plays with my helmet on the floor as if it were the chief among his toys, even better than the xylophone or the old wheel bearing from our 1981 Subaru.

Some parents might think that I'm already setting a bad example for Nathaniel, but even if my risk taking is a vice, I'm pleased that he seems to delight in it. I'm pleased because I want him to see joy in action, and joy for me is a calculated risk. When I climb a tree, he's squinting up at me and bouncing up and down, a cheerleader for himself as much as for me. When, on the big kids' swings, I leap off in mid-swing and land fifteen or so feet away in the sand, he watches wide-eyed and laughs his big belly laugh. Pretty soon, I know, he'll need some instruction in carefulness and judgment, and my risk taking may require some explaining. He'll find a kid's way of emulating some of those risks; others will simply be off-limits to him, the way scissors and tablecloths and plants are off-limits now. But even as he absorbs his daily dose of no, Nathaniel needs an equal, if not greater, dose of yes. The yes is exactly what I want to give him.

A motorcyclist, or a mountain climber, or a parachutist holds his life in his hands, and in that sweet grasp he learns to love who he is, even the limits that define him. Maybe I'm hoping for too much, but I'd like to think that, in a risky world, I am nurturing in my son a self-regard that will be his best defense against danger. An appraising eye and a sense of drama will be his guardians.

In the meantime, I try to keep my own appraising eye in shape. I keep on riding my motorcycle where the roads are narrow and winding, and, even when the risk is greatest, I hear my son's name.

NATHANIEL IS NOW NEARLY FOUR. IMAGINATIVE AND ARTICU-late, he can give me a pretty accurate rundown of the day's events at his preschool. He likes to collect toy spiders, insects, snakes, and dinosaurs. It's funny to think of him standing on a motorcycle gas tank, or whacking the exhaust pipes; that would be kid stuff for him now. When we went over to a local motorcycle dealership the other day to take a look around, he spotted a kid-sized Honda, swung his leg over the saddle, and revved the throttle. He looked like a natural.

So my words are dated. They're dated in other ways, too. I no longer own a motorcycle—at least for the time being. This is partly because my old motorcycle cost more to ship across the country than it was worth, and we had to leave it behind when we came to Massachusetts. But there was another reason—an accident—which left the bike itself with a smashed gas tank and a few jagged edges. As many people regularly remind me, I was lucky to have survived.

There's no doubt that the changes in my life have been immense. Are the words I wrote earlier still, then, my words? Who is that *I*? Certainly not the one writing these words—the professor, husband, father, driver of a ten-year-old Subaru, payer of bills. Lay my earlier opinions about motorcycling on a cold steel table in the morgue of old, abandoned, ridiculed, or socially worthless writing, and call me to identify them—could I, would I do it? Absolutely. For their essential subject—risk and death and generation—has not changed.

All travel involves some risk, and my long journey away from my father, my mother, and their God has been thirty-four years before the mast, on a ship with a jury-rigged rudder and a broken compass. Yet, because God is never a servant to any image or metaphor, the decay of one metaphor may leave room for others: father and mother may vanish in a lightning storm, but at sea other forms of light, strange phosphorescent happenings, may lead the sailor on.

My sister, my brother, and I all found our own versions of these lights. Sibling rebellions struck the family like a light from a masthead, while I found my light under a bushel. From watching John and Cin suffer, I learned—or thought I learned—that certain risks were not worth taking; certain journeys carried the traveler too far from safety. Did I know, then, that I was nevertheless on the same journey as John and Cin? I behaved well because I wanted to keep what I thought of as my freedom. Yet any strong-willed person, despite his desire to conform for safety's sake, will ultimately manifest the qualities of character that make him unacceptable to the status quo. I was, and am, strong-willed, and ultimately I pay the price such self-definition exacts. But I was also docile, and believed that I could hold my world of family and faith together if I simply behaved. Between these two pulls was a kind of empty space, an absence, where for a time as a child I took the risk of creating my own world and found joy in it.

THE EMPTY SPACE OF MY CHILDHOOD WAS THE BEDROOM FLOOR. My family lived then in a great old monstrosity of a house, always on the verge of falling down yet always sturdier than it seemed. The rooms were enormous and, given our minimal furniture, a little barren. My room, however, did have a large rug, and its pale rust color seemed like a perpetual autumn sunset under my feet. It was not a good color to wake up to; on the other hand, the rug was warm and relatively soft, and it made a solid enough foundation for my transient towns and ramparts. For several years I built my miniatures of the imagination—castles and tunnels made of wooden blocks, small farms and cities for Matchbox cars. I knocked them down a few days later with a pleasure almost equal to the pleasure of creating them. Then my mother came back from Venice, and things changed.

I was ten when my mother left on this journey. Although she spent a great deal of her time in an air-conditioned bus, she might well have been Edith Wharton on her first grand tour, so much did the trip mean to her. For years, I knew, she had wanted this; it simmered as a subject on hot summer days in Avalon, New Jersey, and boiled over from time to time in the tedious late winter evenings of Pennsylvania. With one phrase spit out at my father, she would capture her whole life's denial: "If you weren't so tight-fisted" or "You'll be sorry when I'm in Paris"—words which, in the context of her facial muscles tightened as if with a wrench, made her suddenly frightening. She might not speak to any of us for a day or more, until my father came home with a double bouquet of roses and talked quietly with her, and things got back to normal.

It was true: my father, incarcerated in his fear of another Depression, gave little leeway with the money he earned. Ultimately my mother took on part-time jobs—teaching third grade as a substitute, grading high school English papers—to earn enough money for a trip to Europe. It must have taken years to build that sum, and after teaching, or in the evenings as she labored over unreadable essays, she had to cope with my father's complaints about housework or her children's constant intrusions. But, in a moment of unwarranted disbelief years before, my father had said that my mother could go to Europe if she earned the money. She held him to his word.

Those were two long weeks, in which I did not miss her as much as I expected, and missed her far more; but she did come home. My father and I drove from West Chester to John F. Kennedy International Airport to pick her up. On that rainy September evening the clouds brought the darkness down early. We stopped for dinner at a chain restaurant along the highway, where my father ordered only coffee. Though delayed, the plane landed safely, and when my mother emerged from customs she seemed like someone being met just after a great revelation—someone on the down side of a wave. I remember an ambiance of disappointment, but my own joy far outweighed it. We threw her suitcases in the car as she told me about all the trinkets she'd collected for me at different points. I couldn't wait. I climbed into the back, and began to open the suitcase she'd reserved for presents.

"Now wait a minute," my father yelled sternly, but Mom interrupted.

"It's OK, Warry," she said, calling him by a pet name I hadn't heard in weeks. "Let him be."

I found some wonderful things—a Matchbox Opel Cadet I'd been wanting, a Corgi police car with words that didn't quite say "police" ("What language is this, Mom?" "That's Italian, dear"), and some smaller odds and ends. I also found a long, narrow box. In the dim light of the car I held it up.

"Is this for me?" I asked.

She looked back a little longer than necessary. "Absolutely," she said.

At first I could hardly see it; it seemed to be jet black inside, with a little man dressed in white standing at the rear. My eyes and fingers determined the shape at about the same time: it was a gondola, a black wooden gondola from Venice, with two seats—covered with something soft, some kind of felt— and a gondolier in the stern. Before she'd left, my mother had shown me pictures of Venice and its gondolas. I was fascinated. A city on water was too good to be true, a perfect escape (for even then I was fascinated with escape): a series of islands linked with bridges, where narrow canals twisted their intricate paths away from all but the most determined pursuers. And, of course, the whole city seemed to float—neither earth nor air, and therefore not quite human, or rather, better than human. From the beginning I had learned to distrust mortal life; it was only right that I grasped at signs of hope for the more-than-human in this world. And Venice was one of those signs.

Having read my mother's tourist guide to Venice, I knew that my city had to begin with the Piazza San Marco and the cathedral there. What I built, however, was not Saint Mark's. From the first moment I began to cut the cardboard swiped from my father's laundered shirts, I had only the vaguest interest in the real city. I wanted to see, in my room, the passages and the secret places. I wanted my gondola to go there. It did not really matter, then, that after three days of building, my cathedral looked like a cross between a Byzantine chapel and a Norman castle. I did not know Byzantine from Norman from Venetian, nor did I particularly care. What mattered was that my cardboard and scotch tape castle had walls, crenellations, and turrets, and a secret dome where the doomed faithful came in full confidence of their safety. Floating in the middle of my rust-colored rug with the black gondola docked beside it, it seemed a gleaming sanctuary, an island beyond the reach of ordinary miseries. It was magical.

No—not magical. It was the beginning of something, a source of wonder, but at the same time fully within my control. It was the work of my hands. As it sat there for a few days, I began to consider what to do with this sanctuary. A bridge to another island made sense, but what would be on the other island? An outdoor cafe, of course, with little seats and tables by the water. Food, drink, and faith, my three nemeses as a child and the three things for which I yearned, would all be celebrated in this two-island version of Venice.

I made another island by folding a large piece of cardboard into a low box. The cafe turned out to be rather sordid and appealing, with a low roof and a shadowy overhang, and the tables were pure serendipity: my mother had recently bought a dress in a polka-dotted cardboard box, and the dots were table-size. I mounted them on small cardboard pedestals, and cut and taped tiny chairs to go with them. When the cafe was done, I commuted by gondola from church services to long afternoon repasts. But that only whetted my appetite.

Thus began my model-building career, though of course I had no idea of this at the time. Not until 1976, when Stanford abruptly cancelled its architecture program and I began an English major rather than a combined English and architecture major, did I finally give up on the plans I had hatched in my bedroom laboratory ten years earlier. As I created more of my own Venice, however—as I added islands and stores, narrow canals and increasingly ornate bridges—I began to realize something a little jarring about my world: it was no longer a given. It was not something I had to accept, the way I accepted the Scientific Statement of Being from the Sunday school superintendent every Sunday, or the way I accepted praise or punishment from my parents.

"Be ye therefore perfect," I was reminded regularly—not knowing for years that the ancient Greek translation of the original Aramaic did not really mean "perfect" as Christian Scientists used the word, but rather "complete" or "whole." Like the other Christian Science children I played with, I struggled to be "perfect"—intelligent and well-behaved and free from illness—and when I failed, I took this as evidence that I was unworthy of the perfect, finished world that Christian Science offered me.

But, as the architect of my Venice, I saw spreading before me something that flatly contradicted what I heard in church. The world was neither perfect nor finished: here I was, adding to it even as I played. Of course, in some way I had already known this; I knew it whenever I saw a road grader or a backhoe at work. But I had never really applied these observations to *me* before. If my world was neither perfect nor finished—if I could add to it, improve it or detract from it—

then I too was neither perfect nor finished: I was not the purely spiritual being that my religion explained to me. I was someone else, an unknown.

It was at about this time, I remember, that I had dreams of being sucked slowly into an overwhelming, soft, utterly pliant beige ball, something so ordinary and commonplace (the walls of the Sunday school were painted beige) that no reasonable person would think twice about it. It rolled toward me slowly, featureless, and slid up my body until it covered my mouth and nose and I tried to scream but couldn't and awoke in a heated sweat. I cannot divorce the dream from the world of my Venice, which—as it grew and prospered— came to win my love as well as my curiosity.

Over a period of two months Venice grew from two islands to twenty or twenty-five, and ultimately it spanned the entire floor of my bedroom. No one but I could navigate in these intricate waters. I had designed the canals to be wide enough for my feet alone; thus no one else came into my bedroom. For the first time I could remember, I had a definite, calculated refuge. Once I came home from a wearying day of school or an anxious hour of Sunday school, I entered another world, a world of my own making. I knew the day's events on every island. I knew who had bought clothes on the tailor's island, and where he was going with them. I knew which gondola he had taken (by this time I had constructed other gondolas out of cardboard to go with my prized possession, the head of my fleet), and where he had stopped for lunch. Someone robbed a bank in a narrow canal four or five islands away from St. Mark's, and the police gondolas had to set out a dragnet in several different canals. I positioned them so that the robber would just be able to escape to the open sea at the far end of the room. Then he was on his own, as I was. But back in town the bells were ringing in St. Mark's for the evening mass, and people who had gathered for late afternoon coffee in the cafés were summoning gondolas or walking across bridges to reach the great edifice. And somewhere (it changed daily) a small child was playing in a tiny back channel with a rowboat, dreaming of the day when he would pole a gondola on the Grand Canal.

For almost three months, Venice was my home. After that time, the tape began to peel away from the cardboard, and dust took away the sheen from St. Mark's. More importantly, I had run out of room. There was nowhere else for Venice to go. And so I destroyed it—not wildly, as I used to do, but methodically and gently, peeling apart the buildings in whose walls I had invested so much life, stacking the cardboard bridges in a corner and then throwing them out.

I was sad to have reached a limit. On the other hand, there was more to be built, as I knew from a quick glance at the current *Life* magazine. It was almost 1967; Moshe Safdie was erecting his Montreal blockpile, Habitat '67, and I saw immediate possibilities. What kind of shapes could you make with ordinary houses? How far could you go? Safdie had only a few city blocks, but I—in scale, anyway—had acres. How big could Habitat get? That was my next building adventure, which lasted until the World's Fair opened that spring. By then I was bored with Safdie's boxes, and had switched to a kind of cardboard pyramid—much harder to stack, but more of a challenge. In a slightly regressive way, I was growing up.

By this time I knew the textbook answers to Sunday school teachers' questions, and because I earnestly wanted to be good I was successful at pleasing them. It was also necessary to please them, or rather to be pleasing, because my physical well-being depended on my devotion to the religion: to stay healthy I had to be a good student of Mary Baker Eddy, even if I could not find in my heart the truth behind the words I was being taught. The fact that I was a well-mannered Christian Scientist did not mean that I did not want to find this truth; on the contrary, I desperately wanted some consistent confirmation of what I was learning about my relationship to God. Since I did not receive this, I did what I could, which was to behave well. But all of this began to acquire an air of falsity, and when I came back from church I was free to be the maker I had found myself to be.

WHAT DOES MAKING CITIES OUT OF CARDBOARD ON THE FLOOR of my room have to do with riding motorcycles? What do my adventures in architecture and escape have to do with risk? The connection seems to me a strange one, but one that I understood at an inarticulate and instinctive level as a child; only in the last few years have I been able to put it into words. When God was in my life, He was there because I thought of Him. Although it emphasizes spirituality, Christian Science can be a very cerebral religion: when one prays to God, one does not ask God for blessings, but reasons about God's power to eradicate all apparent evils or errors. Even very young children are taught to do this; the recitation of the Scientific Statement of Being at the end of Sunday school is not merely a formality, but a last dose of how-to training, a model prayer for the kids. By meditating on the divine Spirit, and silently arguing for His presence and power, one invokes God in one's life. I would try to do this, as a child, when I was sick or hurt. When I had earaches, for example, or when the metal swing tore into my forehead, I would repeat the Scientific Statement of Being or other passages I'd memorized from Mary Baker Eddy's *Science and Health with Key to the Scriptures* until I was dizzy with pain and exhaustion.

God, for me, was bound up in the process of thinking, reasoning, and trying to open my mind to His mind. Because I was usually attempting to do all this when I was sick or hurt or stuck in some stifling Sunday school, God became the necessary enemy, the presence who would not heal. But when I created Venice or Habitat or some other city on the floor of my room, God was absent. No religious words crossed my brain, and no sense of the unreality of this world confused my awareness of the definite reality of the cardboard and scotch tape I was converting into buildings, sculptures, and boats. When God was absent, I prospered; I gained strength. When He returned, I became feeble, sickly, anxious.

A theologian would quickly point out that my suffering had a great deal to do with language: my sense of God's absence might, ironically, signal the inner presence of a deity far more potent than the one I understood from my early religious training. But I had no one to explain this possibility to me. All I knew was that when I played I took myself away from God. And I was happy. But because I had already learned that human beings could intentionally place themselves beyond God's care—even though God was all-loving—I began to think that perhaps I was a naturally bad child, a truly unreal creature. As I played, created cities, became strong, I began to feel that God's all-loving power did not apply to me.

By then something equally strange had occurred. This was not the tension that existed between my parents, although that certainly seemed strange. My parents, the emissaries of the Father-Mother God, had grown increasingly sullen together. What struck me was that on the rare occasions when they parted for any length of time, each one seemed to gain a surprising strength. It was as if God had grown stronger in division. It was clear, for example, that my mother had opened like a giant heliotrope to the ministrations of the European culture and climate. Even though her return brought an air of disappointment, I could feel her living off her visions of Paris or Nice or Carcassonne for months after the journey. These memories, which she would begin to describe even if no one seemed to be listening, were like a shield around her, protecting her from the ordinariness of domestic tyranny.

Even more striking was the change that had come over my father. At first, when it dawned on him that he would have to take care of me for two weeks alone, he balked. I overheard a dozen conversations in which he professed his inadequacy to my mother. What if I got sick? How would he keep me entertained? What would I do by myself after school? What would we do on weekends? It was clear from these questions how little contact he and I had really had, and in a certain way it made sense: his job was to earn an income, not to play with children. Although my sister was by this time away at college, and my brother was, for better or worse, out of the house most of the time, I was—well, there. Who would take care of me? My mother, who had thought all this out before, pointed out that my school wouldn't even begin until a couple of days before she returned. My father could certainly take two weeks of his vacation time to deal with me. At that point, for just about the first time I can remember, he became an interesting person.

After seeing my mother off at the airport, he returned to Pennsylvania, and we both headed down to Avalon for the remaining ten days of summer. It was quiet there. Although Labor Day had not yet come, most of the summer crowds had gone, and the marinas were beginning to store their fleets of rental sailboats and rowboats. My father, who turned out to be a surprisingly good cook, made a fine breakfast of scrambled eggs and bacon the next morning. Then we went down to his favorite boat yard together to look at some boats and talk with anyone who was still around.

Our old fourteen-foot red motorboat still lay in its slip, rubbing gently against the Clorox-bottle bumpers. I went down to sit in it, swinging its steering wheel around like Ensign Parker on *McHale's Navy,* pretending I was flying down the main channel to Stone Harbor. My father hailed me from the wharf above. He was pointing to the dock where the rental fleet of Sunfish sailboats lay hull up, awaiting winter storage.

"Meet me over there in a minute," he yelled. I shifted into reverse, motored back to Avalon in a few seconds, and hopped out just as he arrived with the owner of the marina.

"You always wanted to learn to sail, didn't you?" Dad asked me. I nodded warily. Sailing intrigued me, but the only time I'd been out before was with my uncle Dick, who heeled his Sunfish to what seemed the brink of capsize while assuring me that nothing could go wrong. I had been petrified. What was Dad thinking?

The marina owner and my father began to turn the hulls over, examining them for cracks and dents. One of them, a sleek porpoise of a hull with a green splashboard, looked remarkably new. But I wasn't sure I was in the mood to go out for a sail.

"How would you like a sailboat?" Dad asked.

"What?"

"A sailboat for you—well, for both of us. I haven't sailed in a long time. We could learn to sail together. You know, this week. Before the summer's all over."

We just stood there, looking at each other.

"You mean you want to *buy* one of these?" I said. "They must cost a fortune."

"Not really," said Dad. "Harvey here is selling these old ones at a pretty fair price." Pretty fair in Dad's language meant a steal. "I just thought we might get one."

"Sure." It was a word I should have regretted, given my past experiences with sailing. But somehow, as I watched Harvey raise the hull in a winch and lower it onto our station wagon, I wasn't regretful. I did not wonder then—as I wondered later—whether the money for the Sunfish might have been better spent on my mother's European journey. Nor was I excited. I was curious—curious to see what this all would be like, and curious to see who this man was behind this new enterprise.

That night he cooked creamed chicken and frozen peas— a dinner I was happy to eat every night for a week—and told me stories about sailing around Avalon as a boy. The night grew close around the house, but we did not go off to our separate rooms, as we usually did. We stayed around the dining room table, and talked, and played cards, and talked a good long time before finally growing tired enough for bed. I slept well that night.

In the morning, we took the Sunfish down to the channel at the end of the street and launched it. It was the kind of

September day that makes longtime residents rejoice in the absence of tourists: warm, sunny, with a light breeze and a few picturesque clouds. Dad rigged the Sunfish, more or less explaining what he was doing and why, and then slid off to hold the boat for me as I got aboard. Then he shoved off. Instantly I was anxious, which—uncharacteristically—he must have seen or felt; he was soothing, and his movements had a slowness or grace to them that I only saw when he worked on machines.

"Let's just take this real easy," he said. "We can just drift into the marsh if we want to. We can always beach the thing and walk home."

A breeze came up, and Dad pulled on the rope, or sheet, to start his tack. We began to heel over. Water ran over the first couple of inches of the deck. I clung rigidly to the gunwale. Then Dad simply let go of the sheet, we slowed down, settled back into the water, and began to drift. We were safe.

"See? That's all you have to do. When the boat starts heeling over, just let the sheet out—let it all the way out if you want to. Or steer into the wind. Both'll take the heel right out of the boat."

I had never known that. I had often seen Sunfish capsized in the harbor, their sailors less than merry in the cold channel water, and I had assumed that a capsize was the unavoidable consequence of being foolish enough to sail in anything more than a puff of air. Now I saw that I was wrong: the sailboat could be controlled. I could control it. It was not a frightening thing.

Dad seemed to be enjoying himself in a kind of aimless way I had never connected with his temperament. We sailed on one tack for a few minutes, with no great attention to heading or speed, then came about and sailed on the other tack. Then we went downwind for a while, the sail swelling slightly at a rough right angle to the hull. It was easy to lose track of time and distance going downwind. We seemed like Frog and Toad on one of their eternal daily outings. When, after a while, Dad looked back and saw how far we had come from the end of the street, he thought we might begin to tack back. This time he handed me the sheet. Now I was in charge, or at least half in charge, of the boat's speed and stability. And we didn't capsize. We had a good sail back to the dock, tacking and talking. He told me about jumping off the high dunes up around Sixtieth Street when he was a kid, and about the icehouse fire many years before, and about the time the water tank overflowed when an attendant fell asleep and forgot to turn off a pump. It was good Avalon lore—some I'd heard before, some was new—but on the sailboat it had a companionable sound, and it seemed to hold us close to this place and this new adventure. We had a good time.

We spent the week sailing, then packed up the house and headed back to Pennsylvania. I vaguely remember starting school; it seemed to cause no particular trauma. I must have been living off the fresh air I'd breathed the week before on the waters of Townsend's Inlet and the main channel to Stone Harbor. When my mother came home, things got back to normal: she was devoted and religious, I was happy to play by myself in Venice, and my father worked long days. But I had seen that division could yield strength, and though I was not sure what to do with this knowledge I kept it with me, like a light under a bushel, until the bushel itself caught fire.

AND THEN I RODE. I RODE A MINIBIKE AND THEN THE BENELLI around the backyard, wearing a rut in the grass and pretending to be a flat-track racer. Later, three thousand miles away, I licensed the Benelli and rode it in the foothills of the Pacific coastal range, looking for a back route to my first girlfriend's house. I had a dream, about that time, of crashing on the highway and seeing my head split open; I did not ride for a while. But after the fear had subsided, I picked the habit up again, this time with a large and powerful motorcycle, and I rode it until the day on a rain-slicked road when I heard the faint sound of asphalt scraping away the side of my helmet as I slid along the pavement.

It was not from perversity that I rode, nor from a simple desire to escape—although escape was what I thought I wanted from an early age. I rode because God was absent. I rode because the act of riding took all of my attention and all of my skill; without these I would die. I heard no divine reasoning in my head. I saw and moved and turned and straightened and saw—not like an advanced machine, an artificially intelligent robot, but like a spiritual animal, a bodily creature fully attuned to his world. And in this absence of all that God had been to me, I began to get the slightest glimmer of what God might actually be.

But there are different ways of riding. In some ways, for me, the motorcycle is the most pure form—the most demanding to mind and body—although other forms come close. At the moment, for example, I'm back at Duxbury beach, where Nathaniel and Lesley and I come regularly to play, but I'm not actually on the beach. I'm about a thousand feet up, in a Piper Warrior, crossing the sand as I head out over the ocean and reduce my altitude to about seven hundred feet. I'm on the downwind leg of a final approach to Marshfield Municipal Airport, where I sometimes fly with Steve Grable, a flight instructor at Shoreline Aviation. It's a bumpy day, and I'm feeling a little queasy, which does not bode well for my progress toward a private pilot's license, but at the moment I'm not really thinking about that. I'm thinking about getting down.

Looking left for traffic, I bank left at thirty degrees and announce our base leg on the airport frequency, 122.8 Mhz. Another left bank, and we're on final. The wind is blowing at about fifteen knots from the northwest, so we can't head in straight; we're crabbing in, flying toward the runway, but aiming into the wind. Full flaps. We're showing 1500 RPM; airspeed's down to about seventy knots. It looks as if we're going to land sideways. I can't yet do this part, and Steve takes over: lower, lower . . . for a moment it all seems peaceful, magical, as if we were hovering over a benign miniature of the real world. A gust catches us just over the runway and we float, now lined up with the center line, now turning slightly into the wind, as Steve fiddles with the ailerons and eases the control wheel back to flare out our glide. Then we're down, solidly, in a stiff crosswind. A good landing.

There is, I admit, something a little frightening to me about flying light airplanes. The fact of being disconnected from the earth jars me, even though statistically it's safer to fly light airplanes than to ride motorcycles. Flying and motorcycling share, for me, a peculiar spiritual revelation: they both silence the God of my childhood. And in that silence I hear the distant tremor of another presence. It's not an idea—barely a voice—but it's near, a turn or bank away, and though it sometimes frightens me with an echo of doom, I still feel it more truly than I ever felt the God of my youth. I ride, and fly, because of that presence. Those are my risks.

But the other kind of riding, the kind I did when I created Venice and Habitat, has a social force—a way of connecting me to the world—that motorcycles and airplanes do not. I did not turn out to be an architect, but my writing became an alternative architecture even when I was in grade school. It ultimately became the greatest risk, the adventure in self-fashioning that led me into an unknown I would have to trust because there was no other route. That kind of adventure requires a self-will equal to the inevitable crises. But it also requires love; it cannot function without love. And this love cannot be spiritualized or abstracted, cannot be cruel. It must begin as a pair of human hands, or a look, or a body that is glad for its bodily life. If my own instinct to pursue God's absence led me away from my childhood constraints, then love—or rather, a few specific people who loved me—preserved me along the way. And that love made it possible for the architecture of my words to mean something. In the absence of God and the presence of love, I began to frame my allegiance to a self I could not yet name.

4

ALLEGIANCES

I DO NOT RECALL EVER HAVING BEEN HEALED OF A PHYSICAL illness through Christian Science. For my minor maladies, for colds and flus and cuts and bruises, my parents called practitioners who comforted them, or me, with prayerful words. Over the course of a few days I improved, and prayer rather than nature received the credit. I accepted the validity of this judgment, despite the tensions in my family, because in some sense the religion was the most stable force in my life. It had a constancy and method that I felt obliged to trust; if I trusted, I would be healed. And the alternative—doctors and the unreal and unreliable medicine they prescribed— seemed too grim to contemplate.

The problem was that on the rare occasions when a chronic illness or injury occurred, I ultimately wound up in the office of one of those suspect healers. Despite my illness, I would cling to my religious roots; this did not ease my difficulties. Why, I wondered, did the doctor's medicine heal me if it was unreal? Did that mean I was also unreal? These thoughts were

too frightening for me as an eight-year-old, when I had bronchitis, and so I pushed them away. I reconciled myself to the
idea that my medical adventure had been an aberration, a
glitch in the scientific system of my religion, and that from
then on I could expect prayer to work and God to heal.

This was not so. I was lucky; I had no significant physical
problems for many years. But when I was a freshman in high
school, I broke my arm playing soccer. In retrospect it was
comical. I was playing goalie because I was too uncoordinated
to play anything else and my team was confident that no one
could score on them. But the other team had a one-man strike
force, and when he was barely eight feet away he took a shot
that would have made Pele proud. It caught my left arm at
the wrist, snapping it instantly. I fell to the ground in agony,
then limped over to the sidelines and knelt into the grass,
cradling my left wrist.

Even then, on the verge of passing out, I was praying—
that is, insisting on God's love and my eternally perfect relationship with Him, as I had been taught in Sunday school.
Both teams gathered around me, and the coach—alarmed at
my sweaty, pale skin—asked one of the other boys to escort
me to the school nurse. This was almost worse than the injury.
I wanted them all to leave me alone, so I could be healed in
peace. Now they were going to drag me into their system,
their unreal system, and I would have to explain that I was
a Christian Scientist and didn't need medicine and they would
cajole and persuade and I wouldn't be able to concentrate on
my praying. I was feeling quite lightheaded. By the time I
got to the nurse's office I was staggering, and the nurse wanted
me to lie down, take an aspirin, and wait for the doctor. I
refused. Instead I asked to call my practitioner. Through all
of this I felt obliged to demonstrate my confidence, since I
understood that God would heal me. When the nurse looked
doubtful, I reached for the telephone with my left hand.

"See?" I said. "I'm fine. I'm going to be healed." As I
grabbed the receiver, my mind went white with pain. I

dropped the receiver and sank down into the chair. The nurse was angry.

"You may continue behaving this way if you wish," she said, standing up, "but I am here to help you, and I cannot stand by and watch you act like this."

She stalked out of the room. It said much about my state of mind at the time that I felt I had scored a victory: I had defeated at least one representative of *materia medica*. In the silence of the unsullied office, I dialed my practitioner with my right hand; when she answered I explained what had happened. Both my mother and father were out of town that day, so I asked her to pray for me and told her I wanted to stay at school. She said she would pray for me.

With the greatest pain, I managed to go back down to the locker room, get dressed, and go to classes. My only difficult encounter that afternoon was with Mrs. Schuessler, my journalism teacher, who pronounced my arm broken and told me I was being stubborn and ridiculous for not seeing a doctor.

"How can you deny what has happened?" she demanded.

"It hasn't happened," I said. "There's a higher reality and you're interfering with my religion."

She looked at me as if I were a lunatic, and left me alone. Again I felt as if I had scored a victory. Despite my shyness and preference for subversion, I could occasionally speak boldly. I'd been aware for many years that Christian Science set me apart, and that people who did not understand my religion were at some level potential enemies. Now I was freeing myself from them, one at a time. Perhaps this was all part of my healing.

When I got home, however, my mother had returned from her day in San Francisco, and she looked at my arm with great concern. After calling my practitioner, and talking with her in a low voice for a few minutes, she emerged from the other room with her purse and keys.

"Get in the car," she said. "We're going to the doctor."

"No way," I said, perfectly and quietly adamant. I had a healing to attend to.

"Mrs. B. said we should do this," my mother countered. (Mrs. B. was our shorthand name for the practitioner.) "If she says we go to the doctor, we go to the doctor."

I was incredulous: I had trusted in God, and human beings were betraying me. Exhausted, sullen, and a little feverish, I went off to the Palo Alto Medical Clinic, where people entirely unlike me practised a form of healing in which I did not believe.

It was an unwanted revelation. The doctors and nurses I encountered neither hovered ominously nor preached their own virtues; they were quiet and solicitous. The way the nurse gently laid my wrist on the table to be X-rayed seemed almost too good to be true. Jim Plunkett, the star quarterback at Stanford, had been in just before me, and the nurse told me some of the jokes he'd told her.

"He's such a sweet guy," she said. "I kept hoping he wouldn't trip or something and, you know, break his arm."

My laughter didn't hurt as much as I thought it would. The physician who wrapped my wrist and applied the cast was an older man wearing ordinary street clothes; he was no one to be afraid of. On the contrary, he held my arm almost tenderly as he worked, and his questions about my life and interests—I was an avid photographer at the time—made me feel oddly appreciated, as if I had done them a favor by coming in. When I refused his offer of painkillers, explaining that as a Christian Scientist I couldn't take drugs, he smiled a gentle smile and said nothing.

THAT WAS IN 1971. I REMAINED A CHRISTIAN SCIENTIST FOR twelve more years, finally withdrawing from the church in 1983. It might seem incomprehensible that after my enlightening encounters with medical healers, I should choose to remain in a religion that insisted on the unique reality of spiritual healing. It is true that, unlike my brother and sister, I had a relatively high tolerance for contradiction and inconsistency. To be subversive means to learn to accommodate the irreconcilable, and I became quite skillful at this. But it wasn't simply a matter of manners, or a fear of losing the Father-Mother God, that kept me in the church. It was something else, something simpler: it was love.

But what was it that I loved? For years this question seemed opaque to me. I loved my family and my church; at least I used the word to describe these relationships. Yet, when they failed me, I had another, different love to fall back on. For many years I did not see it as fundamentally different from those other, more spiritual loves; I gathered them all together in a ragged bundle, assuming their similarity because to assume their difference would have been too troubling. Toward the end of my teenage years, however, I began to see that the one exceptional kind of love in my early life was the love of bodies.

In Plato's *Symposium,* to which I returned repeatedly in college, I was much taken with Diotima's sketch of the soul's quest for the ultimate reality of beauty. The soul, she says, begins by studying the beauty of one body, then two, and then "every lovely body" before moving on to more abstract kinds of beauty. Instinctively, I believed, I had done this too: I had learned to love by loving individual beautiful bodies, even though my religion taught me to spiritualize those bodies and deny their physical reality. It was, however, precisely that physical reality which came to my rescue when I was a child. To that physical reality I gave an instinctive allegiance, although for many years that allegiance could not become conscious.

When I was a little boy, my mother sometimes hired an African-American woman named June to look after me when she was too exhausted or too busy to manage. And June, I knew, loved me. This was somehow different from the Love, the synonym for God, that I studied in Sunday school. When

I was around June, I felt a warm presence, an absolute certainty that the world was secure and that I was cherished. It was clear to my mother that June and I had some special bond. Something in me even brought out a gift of prophecy in June, which impressed my mother for the rest of her life. When I was scarcely a week old (my mother used to tell me) June caressed my head as I lay in the crib and suddenly announced, "His education will be taken care of all the way through college." For my mother, who worried constantly about money and who saw education as at least a potential liberation, June's words carried an ineradicable comfort. Many years later, when it seemed difficult for my parents to afford the spiraling cost of a college education for me, my mother would recall June's words, and trust that something would work out.

As a child, when my mother asked me about June, I could never quite explain my sense of attachment. How could I have explained love in a family where love was too often an abstraction? My mother would observe that June was a very religious woman, and I would understand this to mean that June represented the spiritual value of Love, or God. But this made no sense, for June's love was not like a spiritual value; it was a presence, a physical reality, something that required no thought.

In some ways it seems odd that I found June so comforting, because she was a definite and forthright woman. She said exactly what was on her mind. Her brusque manner contrasted strikingly with my mother's urge to smooth and conciliate; it contrasted with the behavior of most of the people I knew. Accustomed to evasions, I ought to have shrunk from her directness. Instead it drew me to her. When she was tired from a hard day of taking care of me, she never concealed her weariness; she simply sat down. When I teased her or called her names, I knew her anger not by her volume but by her tone. "I'm not going to put up with that," she'd say firmly, and I'd know that without some vestige of an apology I wouldn't have her to play with me for the rest of the day.

I did not always like her, but she was completely reliable: I could trust her responses. My love for her, and my sense of being loved, grew from that trust.

When I was about six years old, my parents went away for a weekend to Cape Cod—a rare luxury for them, a crisis for me. Fearful of the world, unsettled, I clung to my parents, particularly my mother. Their departure left me anxious and angry: I whined and complained, slept badly, and tagged after June. She never yelled, never resorted to the histrionics of my grandmother, yet she made it clear that some kinds of behavior were reasonable and others were not. When she fixed my standard breakfast of bacon and scrambled eggs, for example, she did not whip the eggs as my mother did. With the egg whites only partially blended, little white flecks showed up all over the place. I refused to eat scrambled eggs with white flecks. June took away the offending breakfast, got a whisk from the drawer of utensils, and beat the new eggs until they were smooth and creamy. All the while, however, she talked—not to me, exactly, but to the room.

"Ain't nothin' wrong with white specks," she said. "It's all good egg. Gotta learn to eat it some day. Shame to let good food go to waste."

I ought to have felt guilty, hearing her words, but I did not: her two messages interested me. I had made her angry, I had transgressed her boundaries of good behavior, and she wanted me to know that, but she would not abandon me because of it. I was not a bad child. I was a child who needed care. And she would give it to me, though not without protest.

When, at night in the dark of my room, she held me, and I cried a little, or told her how frightened I was that my parents would never return, she sang songs, or simply told me that I was loved and that things would turn out fine; and I believed her. Her arms were as eloquent as her words. Wrapped in one of her hugs, I felt protected from any disaster. Although, as far as I knew, she went to the same church as my parents, she did not talk to me about God; nor did she read to me from *Science and Health,* or tell me that right thinking was a kind of prayer and that I needed to let myself think correctly, spiritually. Other people did these things, but not June. Sometimes she told stories about people she loved; sometimes she made up stories about animals in the forest or jungle. I lived in her imagination even as I rested in her arms, and felt, for a time, complete.

MANY YEARS LATER, IN 1984, MY FATHER HIRED A REFUSE DIS-posal company to bring a full-size dumpster to the family house in Los Altos. He then gave me a call. He was starting life over with his third wife, he told me, and that meant getting rid of the past—all of the past. I had three days to take whatever I wanted out of the attic or the garage, he explained. After that it would all go into the dumpster, and strangers would pick over it in the seagull-ridden grounds of the local dump.

At that time my wife and I lived one town away, in Palo Alto. We had a one-bedroom apartment and very little money. I was a graduate student at Berkeley, while Lesley was working on her Ph.D. at Stanford. Since my mother's death, we had witnessed my father's increasing alienation from his past. We had always assumed that he would sell the Los Altos house and move away. We had not assumed that he would gut it. Yet it made sense. The only problem was that we had no room for any of the things we wanted to keep. Thus we ran a kind of raiding party, lurching into the attic and garage over the next few days to pick up anything small—boxes of unsorted photographs, a few books, the gondola from Venice, my mother's Bible from her time as Second Reader of the First Church of Christ, Scientist, in West Chester. A few days later, we watched a truck winch the full dumpster onto its flatbed. We saw the old toys and trains, the G.I. Joe space capsule and my mother's old, unfinished paintings. It was like watching the death of a family. And then we left.

What we had, in the aftermath, were pictures. My mother was not a great fan of photo albums, and the several boxes of unsorted photographs from the attic brought surprises: relatives I did not know or had not seen for years, a shadowy picture of my uncle Sandy, and pictures of me. I sat among these pictures one afternoon, noticing patterns. It was striking how often I was photographed alone. Most of the rest of the extended family—Uncle Dick's family, for example, or Naner and her children—always seemed to show up together; even my parents managed to have themselves photographed with friends on the beach in New Jersey. But I was not photographed with friends. I was photographed alone on sand dunes, pushing small sticks that looked like submarines. I was photographed alone in my city of Venice. I was photographed with my skimboard, riding the thin current of water along the edge of the beach.

Where were the other children? Where was anyone? I think back on this, and begin to doubt my whole premise here: what did I know of beautiful bodies? I was scarcely even in my own body; I knew nothing of bodies. I did not like them around me. Instead I had two antidotes to bodies: my own creations, the cities of my heart and hands; and the natural world. These were places where, according to the photographic record, other bodies did not intrude. They were refuges from human ugliness. And somehow, these pictures suggested, I was exceptional: I could discover these refuges or create them, and there, alone, I would be safe and beautiful.

But photographic records are neither reality nor history. They represent the vision of the photographer. In my case, the photographer was more often than not my mother. Was she aware of how often she portrayed me as a child apart? Did that please her, or did it simply reflect the fact that most of the time I played alone? There was something satisfying for her, I remembered, in isolated subjects: as she sorted through the latest packet of prints from the photo store, the pictures she prized made it seem as if only one person were alive at a time on earth. Often I was that person. She lived her isolation through me, but whereas hers was always tentative and broken, mine was often stubborn and uninterrupted. It was true; I lived alone for most of my life. At some point I began to understand that this isolation, like my religion, was crippling. And yet the alternatives, the abject imperfections of human company, seemed—like alternatives to Christian Science—too grim to contemplate.

How, then, could I ever have come to prize beautiful bodies? A child in isolation, who fears other people and learns from the moment he can think that life is not as it appears, may seek and love beautiful bodies because they are strange, they are not like him. They are the other, never defined and never limited; their difference is the starting point of their beauty. This is a somewhat intellectual adult's way of thinking about the matter. As a child I instinctively sought this difference among girls. I loved being around them at school; I loved their furtiveness and outspokenness, loved how they wrestled as well as the boys but also had other ways of fighting.

In kindergarten I tormented one girl (why did I not see this as torment?) by kissing her at the beginning and end of the day for a week. This was not play kissing, I remember, not a dare to see what I could get away with. Who would dare me, after all? I played with no one else. I loved this girl, or regarded her with what I took to be love; something in me even then wanted to be with her, to be her. It may have been a fantasy of possession, or it may have been something else: a longing for release, an escape from the person I was already becoming. After a week, when I came up to kiss her she shoved me away. "My father says that if you kiss me again I should punch you in the stomach," she said. And that was that.

By third grade I was trading phone numbers, talking with girls in the evening for a half-hour or more until my parents or theirs made us hang up. Later, as a teenager overhearing

adult discussions of children, I was amazed at the condescending or dismissive tone that crept into conversations about
childhood love. Adults too regularly doubt the intensity of
their children's feelings. It is not true that children cannot love
or cannot be passionate; they can be profoundly passionate
with each other. But it is not an adult passion, nor is it a
passion that allows adults into its circle. It is something else:
a mystery, a privacy, a source of power.

It may be that the girl I loved in third grade, whose name
was Laura, was an archetypal lover: long, luminous dark hair,
dark eyes, and an urge to escape—a knowledge that the world
of home and school and winter was not the world that could
be. Is there always an anger behind romance, a hatred of all
human systems and limits? Yes, of course. Love and anger
are closely linked; even children know this. Laura and I knew
this as we walked home from school together in the winter,
our breath like a cloud around us as we talked and glanced
to see if we both understood what we were saying.

Much later, when I struggled with sexuality, I remembered
Laura as an ideal of chaste love—not a beautiful body, but a
constellation of beautiful spiritual ideas. I could capitalize
these spiritual characteristics—Intelligence, Grace, Wit, Insight, Humor—and assign them to Laura, so that she became
a set of beautiful values rather than a beautiful individual. At
that point, I told myself, I knew what love was; I had drawn
instinctively on the "innocence" of childhood to love Laura
for her spiritual values.

But this was a lie I told myself in a rather desperate attempt
to draw back from the sexual love that had lured me from
the beginning of my life. In fact, I did not love Laura's spiritual
values; I loved *her*. I loved her body. I loved her look, her
touch on my arm, strong but never presumptuous; I loved
the way she looked away when she talked. I loved her. She
was the starting point, and as I loved her I learned something
about what it meant to be witty and rebellious and angry.
For she was rebellious and angry—angry at her parents, eager
to escape school (how good it was to find someone else who

hated school!), angry to be so young. We talked about Vietnam; we laughed over how we'd had to teach our teacher how to spell it. Since we both had older siblings—my brother was nearly draft age—life seemed electric, risky. We relished that risk. We composed letters to Bob Dylan and Cassius Clay.

And yet, of course, we were both very good children. Her parents put a stop to our telephone calls; they worried that she was becoming obsessed. And they knew I was a Christian Scientist. One day in early spring, she and I walked home in an awkward silence; she would pull away, and return, and slip away again. I could not cross her distance. Finally, a body-length ahead of me, she turned.

"I can't walk home with you anymore," she said. "I'm Catholic. You're a Christian Scientist."

It was an interesting end—interesting in later years—because, in some ways, it was so perfect: a choice had been made for me. I would not have love or desire; I would have religion. And in a way that seemed right, although I could not understand why, in the weeks that followed, I was so miserable. In Sunday school the teachers occasionally told us that Catholics prayed for the destruction of the Christian Science church. My mother repeated this to me at home. I thought it had to be true. Laura's family was Catholic; I had thus been in danger when I was with her. I had been subject to what Christian Scientists call mental malpractice—the attempt by one person or group of people to think thoughts that will harm another person's life. *Mental malpractice*—the phrase haunted me for years, nurturing my unstated awareness of the dark, paranoic side of my religion. In this case, however, I had been saved. Laura's family could not harm me. I should have been grateful—and was, inasmuch as any eight-year-old can be grateful. I was abject. I was also deeply unhappy. There was something ridiculous about the whole scene, and the only people who were left with nothing were Laura and I. We looked at each other across the classroom, mute and muzzled.

Though I did not realize it, Laura was the beginning of a different kind of allegiance for me. My split with her, as minor as it may have been, established a strange pattern in my life: I saw that one gave up love for religion, for principle. And yet religion *was* love. Love was one of the seven synonyms for God in Christian Science, along with Life, Truth, Mind, Soul, Spirit, and Principle. God was Principle; God was also Love.

It did not occur to me at the time I was learning these synonyms that love and principle could conflict, and yet they already had. Love was a drawing out in my life; principle was a drawing back. In love, I was connected to my own talents and to other human beings; in principle, I was isolated. The principle of my religion was a vision of a perfect world; love was a vision of the world as it was. On Sundays, or when I was sick or hurt, someone would read the Lesson-Sermon and pray for me, and then—in theory—my life would become congruent with the harmony of the divine. That was the principle; in my heart I knew that it was not like love. Yet, because love and principle were synonyms in my life, I had for years no vocabulary to explain my divided allegiances. I did not even really perceive a division. Instead, I followed my instinct for beautiful bodies, and called them the names for God.

THE PHRASE *BEAUTIFUL BODY* IS BORROWED, I REALIZE, FROM William Butler Yeats: "All dreams of the soul," Yeats writes in "The Phases of the Moon," "end in a beautiful man's or woman's body." The beautiful bodies in my life were beautiful not because they looked a certain way but because they brought something essential out of me. They compelled me to love them, and thus to love myself. They put an end to my dreaming; they *were*. This was nothing if not an aesthetic response, a proof that beauty was fundamental to any real harmony in life. But I did not think about that especially, not then. I knew simply that when I had found someone or something beautiful, I could give it my allegiance; I could breathe and grow strong in its presence. I did that most strikingly in my early life for two years—from the time I was ten until I was almost twelve—with a small, dark-haired girl who, like me, had transferred from the public schools of West Chester to the difficult, eclectic, catalytic Friends Community School.

Her name was Leslie. Perhaps in some sense she was my wife's forerunner, as my friends sometimes jokingly allege. Why is it that now, as I roll back into my life with her, I find myself suddenly nervous and grasping for words? I cannot picture her. Yet a picture comes to mind, or rather a home movie. In jerky, 8mm frames, Leslie and I are walking across a park in West Chester. Our backs are to the camera. It is the annual May fair; the park is festooned with booths and bean-bag tosses and rope climbs and ferris wheels, and the fire trucks from the local station draw their usual huge crowd at the far corner. Leslie has come over to the park for the day to be with me. We walk hand in hand down toward the basketball courts, where the best booths are. I am wearing my usual corduroy pants and a light, short-sleeved shirt; she is wearing a pale green dress with a floral print, rather Venetian, and her short black hair dusts her shoulders with a crisp, inquisitive precision.

The film itself is gone, a casualty of my father's domestic decimation, buried now under tons of rotting food and cans and microwave trays in a dump in California. But my mind is a fine projector: as we walk we slip for a moment into darkness under the shadow of a large maple. Then, suddenly—knowing all the time that we are being filmed, clumsily oblivious—we turn around. I cannot see our faces.

I go back to words, which themselves are distant from her. My words are literary; she was not. To make her less literary would be to take her out of the abstractions, out of the old home movie, and have her walk with me again through the

times that showed how her love, her beautiful body, changed
me. And yet, when that old 8mm movie runs out and the
trailer flickers through my brain, a darkness descends. There
are no more episodes. I cannot seem to make her real.

I get up, go to the living room, rummage through the high
shelf of dusty books. It's there, my yearbook from sixth
grade, a simple affair with mimeographed pages and pictures
of the students pasted in. It is seventeen pages long. I flip it
open, starting from the rear, where the memorial essays and
prayers appear. Mary Stepler wrote the history of the school.
I'd forgotten that the composer Samuel Barber attended, as
did Andrew Wyeth's brothers and sisters, Ann, Carolyn,
Henrietta, and Nathaniel. A school for artists and artists' families; did I understand that when I was a student? Patricia
Supplee wrote an essay on archaeology, Valerie Rabin on
"The Story of the Old and New St. Augustine" (an auspicious beginning: "On August 28, 1565, Don Pedro Menedez
sighted a coast."). I wrote the valedictory address. Leslie
wrote the class prayer.

I linger over this prayer for a moment, hoping for images.
"Our Heavenly Father, . . ." Nothing comes. The prayer is
standard. Then it shifts: "Help us to have understanding and
love for all people so that prejudice and injustice are abol-
ished." Another curtain goes up in my memory: I am sitting
on stage at commencement on June 12, 1968, the day after
my birthday. The lights shine brightly in my eyes. Leslie is
reciting the prayer on center stage. The auditorium is silent,
and most of the other kids on stage with me have bowed
their heads. I am watching her. She slouches a little, as I do
when I stand, but there is something stubborn and even defiant in her posture. Her hair is beautiful. And there is something even more remarkable about this occasion: this is, I
suddenly recall, a moment of triumph for her.

In the last week of school she had to rewrite the prayer
several times, finally refusing to remove the passage about
prejudice and injustice. I remember her sense of outrage, her
desire that commencement not be just another ritual; she

defended her prayer passionately. I hear Leslie reciting her prayer, and see her as I saw her in my parents' movie, from the rear. It is as if I am looking at myself. Martin Luther King, Jr., has been assassinated; Robert F. Kennedy has been dead scarcely a week. Racial hatred and despair rise from the landscape like a mutant summer harvest. And we are praying Leslie's prayer.

Now I slowly turn the pages, going backward through the alphabet, through time. The glue from the pictures is starting to rot the paper underneath. Will this yearbook survive even my own lifetime? I see the names and faces I lost when my family moved to California: Tacie Yerkes, daughter of the science teacher; Stacey Shreiner, good at everything; Ellen Rutherford; Sally Robertson; Michael Jordan . . .

In the first instant, as always, I find Leslie's face uninterpretable. Is she happy, or is she about to cry? Is she the only one with her hair slightly askew? And whose eyes are those? Are they hers, or mine? The photograph, as minimal as it is, pours out questions. And then I realize why it is I cannot remember this Leslie more clearly, cannot remember a series of incidents like those with Laura. There was, for more than two years, a seamlessness to our time together: when we were together, it was as if we were twins, related not by blood but by the spirit. We knew this because we held hands, saw the truth in each other's eyes, took comfort in our combined physical aura or magic. We each knew what the other thought with no words exchanged; we protected each other. When one of the other boys recklessly swung his stick and hit Leslie on the chin during co-ed field hockey, I started a petition to have him removed from the school. He hated me for the rest of the year, as well he might, although he must have had some satisfaction in the public humiliation I received from the principal. Nevertheless I stuck by what I had done.

Looking into her eyes now, I see that old depthlessness— that stare that could frighten other classmates or make them convulse with laughter. It is still there in the picture. She taught me to live with that stark beauty, brought me into it whether I was cross or sick or depressed or delighted or proud. We girded each other, so that in school we were virtually inseparable. We dreamed about each other at night. To remember her life is to remember mine; they seem too entwined to distinguish, and what emerges is not a series of incidents or even memories, but a sequence of shimmering pantomimes on a dark stage.

It seems odd to realize that, outside of school or special occasions like the May fair, I rarely saw Leslie. She did not come over to my house to play—virtually no one did—and somehow I did not miss that. Once at home, I was in my refuge; I needed no one else.

By the time I was in sixth grade, I had outgrown my architectural room and shifted my allegiance to motorcycles. Hurrying home after school, dropping my books on the bench near the door, I would change into old clothes and run down to the basement, where I played with my brother's old Suzuki and Triumph and, a few months later, with the Benelli. Home was my world apart from knowledge and intellectual learning; it was the preserve of my imagination. And yet, unlike anyone else in my life at that time, Leslie was somehow equal to that refuge. She did not draw me away from it, but she drew a reality out from it to herself. Trust me, she seemed to say, I will not destroy your preserve.

I believed her, but I also became aware of something else as the months went by: I became aware of *her,* of her uniqueness and bodily presence, and of my own desire for it. This was not a sexual desire, exactly, but it emerged from my early fascination with difference, and from the kind of energy and happiness I felt in my own body when I was with her.

On weekdays I went to school, read biographies of Abraham Lincoln and Clara Barton, painted pictures, raised fruit flies, failed multiplication, botched French—and hung around with Leslie. After school I went back to my own shining cities, or to the engines in the basement. At Sunday school, my comrades and I competed to name the books of the Bible in order and listened as the teacher explained our own spiritual perfection. Sin was unreal, but it was unwise for us to sin; bad thoughts and deeds were "errors" which separated us from our divine reality. What were bad thoughts and deeds? Anything pertaining to the body—excessive eating, drinking, or fighting—and anything that showed a strain of disobedience. "Honor thy father and thy mother," said the teacher solemnly, and we understood this to mean not only our earthly fathers and mothers but the Father-Mother God. The words did not go by us, but we could not quite believe them. Sometimes, after Sunday school, some of the other kids and I would have a few minutes before our parents gathered us up for the trip home. We'd talk—the same things each week.

"Think you'll get sick if you say 'goddamn?' "

"Sure you will—that's error."

"No way—my brother says 'goddamn' all the time and he never gets sick."

"Goddamngoddamngoddamn!"

"That's it for you, man—you're a dead man, gonna be sick all week."

"He can't be a dead man, 'cause 'matter is the unreal and temporal.' "

"My grandpa died last year."

"My brother smokes dope."

"Man, he's still in Sunday school!"

I must have been saner then than I am now, or perhaps wiser; these conversations made perfect sense to me, except when I was genuinely sick and terrified that I would not be healed. It may have been a kind of defense against this periodic terror that made me mock my religion, as my companions in Sunday school did. This mockery was the teflon that enabled me to slide over what now seem to be obvious inconsistencies between my passionate love for beautiful bodies and my religion. Although they were not my friends, my Sunday school cohorts were a buffer. Their affected nonchalance allowed me to keep Sunday school somewhat separate from my daily life—at least on the surface—and I could go about

my passionate business without worrying about the dichot-
omy of matter and spirit. I simply loved—or so I thought.
The truth was more ominous. Both Leslie and my religion
were too real to question; thus, in my twelve-year-old mind,
they simply did not conflict.

APRIL 1969. I AM LYING IN BED SHAKING. I HAVE ALREADY
thrown up once; I cannot eat. I thrash around in bed, as fan-
tastic images of dismembered teachers and students leer at
me, and monstrous books surround me until I cannot breathe.
I do this almost every morning; I miss two or three days of
school each week. When I do manage to get to school, I shake
there like a boy in the freezing cold. I try to smile politely at
the teachers, who on the whole seem to ignore me. Only my
English and art teachers give me an occasional hug, or let me
lie down in their classrooms when the other students have left.

Although I cannot explain what is happening to me, I know
that school has become a nightmare from which I cannot
escape. Most of my friends at Friends Community School,
including Leslie, went on to public junior high schools. I,
however, marked for some unnamed success, went on to a
Quaker-affiliated preparatory school in the country some distance from West Chester. Since I began, in September, I have
arrived at school around eight-thirty and have almost never
left before five o'clock. The boys have mandatory soccer practice, even in the middle school (soccer is a passion here), and
my ride home is usually late. When I get home, I have three
hours of homework in math or history or language. My math
teacher seems incapable of explaining the slightest difficulty,
and my parents do not understand this new approach to
algebra.

Food is also a problem. We are not permitted to bring
lunch from home, and the meals we are offered in the school

dining hall are often appalling: scrapple, watery shepherd's pie, hamburgers with foul-smelling meat. Among the stronger students, lunch is simply an adventure or a joke. When one of the eighth-graders finds someone's retainer (not his own) in his slice of apple pie, he holds it up to the applause and laughter of the assembled diners. For me, however, lunch is an exercise in nausea, and I do not eat. By mid-afternoon I am quite faint.

The school prides itself on the accomplishments of its students, and accomplishment means discipline and scholastic excess. I respond to this kind of pressure, of course, in a particularly destructive way, although I do not understand this. Since I have always made myself palatable to other people by being an exceptional student, I naturally must excel here. This means that from the time I wake up until I go to bed around ten o'clock, I am pursuing the goals of the masters and teachers who exhort me during the day.

And yet I do not succeed. My grades are fine; at the end of the year, even though I miss many of my classes in May and June, I still share top academic honors with Skip Armstrong, the acknowledged master of the class. But I do not belong at this school. I am too small, too uncoordinated, too quiet. My parents do not make enough money. I am artistic. For all these reasons I am a target. Three kids grab me in the urine-scented hall, mace me in the eyes with Binaca. The pain brings tears, which they mock. Danny walks up to me one day between classes. "I have a surprise for you," he says. "Hold out your hand and close your eyes." I do, and gasp from the intense burning in the center of my palm. Danny has driven a pencil deep into my hand. I pull the pencil out— the graphite breaks off and because I do not go to doctors it remains in my hand—and wrap the wound in a handkerchief so no one will see. I cannot tell the teacher, or Danny and his friends will find an occasion to make me remember my transgression.

I survive this for months; then odd things begin to happen. I cannot concentrate. I begin to shake uncontrollably at school. I become nauseated in the morning, then at night. The nightmares of my sleep do not vanish during the day. I seem to hallucinate horrible creatures and old terrors; the pliant beige ball of my childhood nightmares returns to haunt me whenever I close my eyes. I cannot go out in any crowded public setting. Even a ride in the car leaves me trembling.

One of the advantages of growing older, if one does not become too bitter, is the experience of looking back with tenderness and knowledge on oneself as a child. I was having a nervous breakdown. I did not know it, and no one around me knew or would admit to it. My parents seemed to think I was simply overtired or "growing." But my own tendency toward academic excess, and the difficulties I faced daily in and out of class, made my mind spiral down upon itself. I could find little humanity at school in 1969; there was no place to be a beautiful body. I saw plenty of competitive bodies, and fine minds—but little beauty.

This was profoundly ironic considering the location of the school. The school commanded some of the most beautiful acreage in eastern Pennsylvania; its forests were rich and dark, its lake overlaid with an unscholarly quiet. Beyond its main gate lay a wide apple orchard, and beyond that—through a hole in the fence—a beautiful meadow ran away from the school and out into open country. I would not have known this, I think, except that in early winter my drafting teacher suffered a massive heart attack and left the middle school without its usual early afternoon class. For the first time in my life I believed in divine retribution: the man had been a tyrant. He cuffed us and verbally abused us, and he once threw me out into the snow without my jacket because he thought he'd heard me whistling—the cardinal sin in his class. I was quietly glad when, finally, he died. I was also grateful because his absence left a free period in my day. For reasons I never understood—and never wanted to question—the school did not try to slip us into other classes. Instead it left us free to roam the library or the woods.

I sometimes went over to see the art teacher, Tania Boucher, the only luminous creature I could discover at the academy and, coincidentally, a friend of the artist Tom Bostelle. If I were feeling sick, she would let me lie down in the classroom and gaze up at the mobiles; this soothed me. Equally soothing were the upper school girls, who had more unstructured time and thus occasionally came in to work on projects. Perhaps because they were dedicated to their own work, laboring from an inner impulse that I had almost lost, I loved them in a somewhat disinterested way. Being among them was like being in a painting from the Northern Renaissance.

More often I would find myself in the orchard or the meadow. No one went there in the winter. The snow hung undisturbed from the apple trees, and when I left the orchard reluctantly, my footprints were the only ones I saw—except for those of the rabbit and the fox. Going down into the orchard on a winter's day was a descent into darkness, for a stand of trees near the barbed-wire fence cast gloom over the snow. It was like going into the grave. But what a beautiful grave—how quiet, how untouched by human hands! And then, with a practiced dexterity, I separated the strands of the barbed wire and eased myself through. I came out the other side, into the clear, pale light of the winter meadow.

The meadow remained my refuge well into the spring. When I managed to get to school, I would make it a point to spend as much of the day as I possibly could along the banks of the narrow stream that further divided one side of the meadow, and the school, from open country. One day I saw motorcyclists racing across the hills a half mile away. I wanted to go home, get the Benelli, and join them. Once with them, whoever they were, I knew I would never stop until I was somewhere else—someone else.

But the meadow was simply an emergency measure, the equivalent of the lunar module on Apollo 13. The minute I set foot out of the meadow, I would begin another round of trembling and nausea, and the horrors that beset me day and night would return. Thus, later in the spring, when my parents could not quite deny that something was wrong with me, I began my occasional visits to my mother's Christian Science practitioner.

It has always been unclear to me how my mother found her, although I tried to take comfort in the fact that she was an official practitioner, listed in the *Christian Science Journal*. I recall her mostly as a large, square, stern, glowering woman stuffed behind a large desk in a very small office. Her bulk, or perhaps her demeanor, made everything around her look tiny. My mother had mentioned to me, before my first visit with this woman, that she had sent her son to a military academy. For some reason this impressed my mother as an act of courage and good parenting. I took it as a double warning: my mother could no longer tolerate my condition, did not wish to consult a doctor, and was desperate for a solution; the practitioner's disciplinarian response to her own son might be in my future as well. I was thus not predisposed to like this practitioner, but I also was desperate, and hoped—despite all negative intuitions—for healing.

On our first visit, the practitioner sat me down across from her and asked me if I knew what it meant to take the Lord's name in vain. I thought of protest signs recently in the news.

"You mean things like 'God save us from Vietnam'?" I asked.

"No," she said with annoyance. "I mean swearing. Do you swear?"

It became clear, then, that our first visit was to be devoted to the moral weakness of my dirty mouth. It was true. I did swear from time to time, and my mother, racking her brains for some reason why I was suffering, must have reported this moral lapse to the practitioner. She, in turn, had determined that I would only be healed of my mental anguish if I were first healed of the need to swear. I was only then becoming alert to what I later described to myself as a form of sadism in Christian Science: the tendency to link physical or mental ailments to moral issues as defined by the conventional Victorian outlook of Mary Baker Eddy. At this moment, however, I simply felt that no matter how crazy I was becoming, this practitioner was crazier. And yet I was trapped. This was the person who was supposed to help me. I listened to her politely, promised to watch my mouth, and went back outside, where my mother was waiting in the car.

"How was it?" she asked me. "You seem better. Isn't she wonderful?"

"She's just fine," I lied, and we drove home.

Fortunately for me, however, an economic matter forced the issue of my health. The practitioner required payment for each treatment, whether in person or over the telephone. After a number of these treatments, I was, if anything, worse. When the common sense streak in my mother won out, she stopped paying the practitioner and stopped sending me to her. Over the course of the next couple of weeks, as I dutifully tried to go to school and came home shaking and incoherent, she hit upon a remarkable idea. Somehow she had noticed that I particularly liked one of my substitute Sunday school teachers, Minnie Murray. It was true: Mrs. Murray occupied a kind of shrine at the far edge of my consciousness, where hopeful possibilities still appeared like mirages from time to time. Mrs. Murray, it turned out, was studying to be a practitioner. Would it be acceptable, my mother said, if she asked Mrs. Murray to pray for me?

And so, years after June cared for me, I found a second beautiful body in Christian Science. Though as old, or almost as old, as my parents, Mrs. Murray was a world apart. Her dark skin and gentle motions radiated a living peace, and when she came over from time to time to see me in person, I felt as if love, finally, had descended upon our house. Out of her mouth came, not lectures or speeches, but questions: how was I doing, how did I feel, what made me happy or unhappy? Rarely did anyone ask me my opinion about anything, even though I think that at some fundamental level my parents were sensitive to my desires. My parents did not know how to listen; Mrs. Murray did. And when she listened, her eyes followed me with a gentle acuteness that made me feel firmly supported, upheld. My body relaxed; I first stopped trembling in her care. I could take deep breaths. And when she recited to me words from *Science and Health,* they did not sound like the words I had heard in Sunday school or had read myself; they had an immanence, an evanescent identifiable reality in the room. I loved this woman, and as I loved her presence—rather than any idea or prayer she provided—I seemed to love myself and to see possibilities in the world where before I had seen only darkness.

Mrs. Murray did not heal me of my collapse; my symptoms did not abate for another year. But I firmly believe she held me together. Her love not only protected me from the incomprehensible distance of my parents and of the other practitioner, it lifted me out of the world of my school. Of course I finished the year there. Yet Mrs. Murray convinced me that divine Love—God—had given me an inviolable identity that no condition in the world could dissipate or harm. I did not have to do well in school. I did not have to behave like the other kids, or even tolerate them. If divine Love led me to be a motorcyclist, I should be a motorcyclist; if divine Love led me to take a walk in the meadow rather than go to class, I should do that.

Through Mrs. Murray's own love I first began to glimpse what divine Love might be, and how powerful its reality could be. It could transform my life. It could liberate me from all the idiotic rules and systems that hampered me. And it could do this in a way that would make me strong. I ultimately survived the class conflict and intellectual strain at school by simply ignoring them: God had wrapped a cloak of love around me which nothing but love could penetrate. Though my faith faltered from time to time, Mrs. Murray never faltered. Sitting across from her in our darkened living room on a late afternoon, I thought sometimes I could see a radiance rising from her body. I knew, then, that Jesus had been a human being, and that love was first and foremost a love of bodies. I did not say it this way to myself at the time. I still talked about Spirit and Soul as I gave thanks for the physical reality of Mrs. Murray. It was not necessary to make distinctions between the abstract and the physical. My sense of relief was what mattered.

"AND THE LORD WENT BEFORE THEM BY DAY IN A PILLAR OF A cloud, to lead them the way; and by night in a pillar of fire, to give them light; to go by day and night: He took not away the pillar of the cloud by day, nor the pillar of fire by night, from before the people." I pause for a moment, turn a page, close the book. No longer do I read the Bible daily, but I hold this passage from Exodus in my visceral memory. I read it with Mrs. Murray in 1969, and as I prayed with her I came to believe that a pillar of cloud would lead me too; that was all I would need.

I was not the only one in the family to need a pillar of cloud. My father's job, which he had slogged through with admirable diligence for over a decade, was becoming intolerable. His evening moods were explosive. My mother was alarmed at his misery, alarmed at my collapse, alarmed at my brother's increasingly dangerous life.

My brother was at that time declaring his conscientious objection to the Vietnam War. The Selective Service System looked relatively favorably on conscientious objectors who had the support of their churches; it looked with equal disfavor upon those who had no religious affiliation, or whose churches did not recognize the CO status. Since the Christian Science Mother Church did not at that time officially recognize conscientious objection, it seemed likely that my brother would be turned down and sent overseas despite his pacifism.

When I read my brother's thirty-page essay outlining his beliefs, I knew—perhaps for the first time—that I was dealing with a formidable and stubborn mind. I had not taken him for a pacifist, for obvious reasons; now I saw another side to him, committed and sincere. It may have been the first time I realized that I loved him. But he stood a good chance of being shot to hell in a Vietcong-controlled rice paddy, like many other sincere young men.

It seemed as if, by the early summer of 1969, we were all adrift. Mrs. Murray kept me going; I do not know what preserved my mother and father and brother. As usual, my mother and I vanished to Avalon for the summer months, seeking shelter from the rigors of Pennsylvania. It helped somewhat. But in my bad times by the ocean, when I walked for hours by myself along the shore, I found myself meditating on the pillar of cloud, wondering if somehow such a pillar might lead us all out of our familial misery. As I read Exodus, I envisioned the stratocumulus cloud and the extravagant fire, and saw those as physical realities, as bodies. They comforted me, as Mrs. Murray did.

One sunny day, as I played in the surf, I heard someone yelling down the beach. Looking back toward my mother, I saw someone—my father—running toward her. He was waving something in his hand. It was a weekday, and his presence in Avalon could only mean that some catastrophe had finally descended. I raced from the water back toward them, instantly out of breath from a rising panic.

Yet as I drew closer, I saw that my father's face was not contorted in misery or fear. He was delighted; he was laughing. He was leaping up and down on the beach. I had never seen such a display of joy from him. My mother, slightly embarrassed, tried to calm him down. "What is it, Warry?" she kept saying. "What is it? Stop that, and tell me what it is."

It was a letter from Ampex, a California company which manufactured magnetic recording tape and technologically advanced recording equipment for professional music studios. They were offering my father a job.

We all sat around staring at the letter, my father and I breathing hard, not saying a word. California! It was a land of stereotypes and fantasies for us, a country of badlands and movie actors. I had once seen slides of Yosemite National Park at Friends School; Leslie and I called it "Yose-*mite*," rhyming it with *dynamite,* until the teacher threatened to throw us out of class for disrupting her show. Part of my problem was that Yosemite was like nothing I had ever seen: too big, too beautiful. It was unattainable, and therefore boring. But as we sat on the Avalon beach in the east-coast sun, I thought of Half Dome, and the Merced River, and Yosemite Falls again, and wondered if I would go there.

It is possible to think of our move to California in many ways: as a series of coincidences, as good luck, as a result of my father's perseverance and patience. But we did not think of it in any of these ways. For us, the move to California was a straight parallel to the Israelites' exodus from Egypt. We had been faithful, and this was our healing. The pillar of cloud and pillar of fire before us turned us west; we were being called to a place that would restore us to health. Love, which I then equated with God, was in the air, in my body, in the world in which I moved; it surrounded me. And it was neither passive nor detached. It directed my life. I was to be freed. It was impossible to think of the move to California in anything but Biblical analogies. The sense of deliverance was too strong.

Which was a good thing, because the move itself was terrifying. Both my mother's and my father's families had east-coast roots going back one or even two hundred years. They were aghast that we might cross the country, especially when, to their way of thinking, it was not strictly necessary. Only fortunetellers and criminals and wayward mothers and people down on their luck deliberately moved west, they told us half-jokingly. How could we do this?

That question resonated in all our minds as the reality of the most daring yes in my father's and mother's life sank in. Our seventy-year-old neighbor, Mr. Hoopes, the owner of the only wagon wheel company left in Pennsylvania, came over from time to time just to talk. On these occasions he really had nothing more to say than the obvious. "I can't believe you're doing this," he would repeat to no one in particular. He was not senile, he was simply stunned.

Complications slowly rose from the move like a host of Pharoah's troops. One house in California cost more than both of our east-coast houses, our run-down house in Pennsylvania and our cottage in Avalon. These were already heavily mortgaged; the question of how to afford to live in California suddenly became almost insurmountable. At a midsummer dinner, when we had all gathered in Pennsylvania to discuss details of the move, my father left the table in tears. His fear and sense of loss frightened me; I was not to understand fully until nineteen years later, when I left my own dinner table in California in tears because I was destined to return to the East.

The stark reality of the move ultimately frightened us all. On the morning of our departure, I could scarcely climb into the car for the trip to the airport. I was shaking as badly as I ever had at school. I knew in my heart this was all wrong. I was going to a place that would destroy me, when to be safe all I had to do was cling to the present and the East.

Sometimes fear can make the heart untrustworthy. This was one of those times. When our airplane landed six hours later in San Francisco, and I looked around me at the dry hills (I thought they were mountains) surrounding the airport, I felt a tremor of attachment, as if I already had roots here that I had not yet discovered. The pillar of cloud had brought me here, in spite of my doubt, through the love of a beautiful woman and other bodies and machines along the way. Now, here, I might—I felt in the heart that had been wrong a few hours earlier—I might start over, breathe a different air, run.

Whatever its cause, there was no greater healing in my life than this move to California. The least of its consequences was a restoration of my faith in Christian Science. I rededicated myself to the religion, attending Sunday school faithfully in gratitude for my exodus. And, as I rededicated myself, I began slowly to work back into the world of abstractions that had comprised my earlier experience of Christian Science. Love slowly faded; right thinking returned.

But not all love faded. A new kind of love sprang up, descended directly from my earlier love of beautiful bodies. This was a love of words, those sounds that formed in my throat and mouth and pleased my mind; it was also a love of place, an infatuation with landscape that I had never really known in the East. I came to love the fragrance of California, the inescapable canopy of its manzanita and eucalyptus. The scent of laurel in the coastal range mingled with the damp density of fog; underfoot the earth crumbled with a loamy crispness that inhered in mind like what Wallace Stevens called "a new knowledge of reality." I felt consistently at home in the physical world for the first time in my life. My love for the girls who became my liberators in high school extended from these early encounters with the landscape of California and the landscape of words.

Yet a kind of knowledge interposed itself between these two encounters. I learned, more clearly than I ever had before, that words meant risk and breakage and loss. This was the beginning of formal knowledge for me. It came at the hands of a brilliant high school teacher named Warren Wilde. Wilde guided my expulsion from whatever garden of Eden I might still desperately have clung to. Yet Wilde offered a great consolation: he validated my love for bodies, and my love for words. Through him I began my second life, the life of a poet.

5

MOURNING

I**T IS EARLY MORNING IN** B**OSTON.** A**S** I **LOOK OUT MY WINDOW**
I can see the long shadows sliding across our neighbor's
brown-shingled triple-decker. I've taken Nathaniel to preschool, and Lesley has gone to the Boston Public Library to
continue her research on nineteenth-century American painting. The house is quiet; all its rooms are full of space in which
to think. As I try, now, to piece together my own visceral
sources of knowledge, I find myself returning to the poems
and poets who have long inhabited my life.

From the first days I studied it with Warren Wilde, poetry
was a refuge. It was a form of speech in which I could explore
my unarticulated love for bodies. It was thus also an escape
from the spiritualized world of my religion. In poetry I could
begin to explore a form of knowledge that I could not, strictly
speaking, acknowledge as real in Christian Science. Yet, because the study of poetry was an integral part of my high
school education, and because Christian Science prized education, I did not necessarily face an irreversible break with

my religion. Poetry was the chrysalis in which I began to learn that I had a self different from the self I acquired through faith and constancy. It was the means by which I began the arduous process of re-creating myself.

My first encounter with Wilde, an English teacher at Los Altos High School, was not particularly auspicious. As I sat at my regulation desk in the fall of 1971, wondering whether I would be named editor of the high school paper later that day, a short, thin man surged into class with an entourage of turbulent air. Some people have an instantaneous presence, a spirit or aura which even thoroughly rational people sense. Wilde was one of these. It did not hurt, of course, that he was dressed entirely in black—black shoes, socks, tight-fitting pants, and a black turtleneck. He had slicked his black hair back flat against the sides of his head; otherwise he was virtually bald. The black frames of his glasses hovered around exceedingly dark eyebrows.

"My name is Warren Wilde," he said, inscribing it with a flourish on the blackboard. "I am here because you are philistines, and it is my job to attempt to turn you into thinking, feeling human beings in a little less than a year. This is probably an impossible task, but I will do it, and I expect your entire cooperation."

He went on for a while, but I found myself lost in outrage over those words. I, a philistine? He had never even met me; he did not know what I thought or felt. I found myself rising in anger against his prejudice, vowing to resist him. I had not come all the way from Pennsylvania to be subjected to another round of academic punishment.

Yet, as I silently pondered my anger and watched him lecture us, I found I could not quite relegate him to my small crucible for worthless teachers. Something about his body belied his words. His movements and gestures across the front of the classroom, though passionate, were not accidental or random. They had a studied grace to them. I had heard rumors of Wilde's training in classical ballet; now I simply found myself caught up in the language of his body. Though his words were critical and supercilious, his body manifested a sensuous centeredness. As he danced across the front of the room, never stumbling or faltering, his thin limbs sliced the air in dark waves. A still, small voice echoed in the back of my head, telling me that Wilde knew something about a vivid life that I needed to acquire. I could not quite believe this in the early fall; I treated Wilde cautiously, as I treated anyone who hinted at condescension, but I did not reject him. Everyday in class, as he talked about the assigned reading and asked questions, I watched him dance.

Over the summer Wilde had had us read W. Somerset Maugham's *The Razor's Edge,* in which the protagonist, Larry Darrell, comes back from World War I with a profound horror of life. The deaths of men at war have convinced Larry that only a concentrated effort will save him from the essential meaninglessness of existence. At the same time, because concentrated effort translates too easily into the Protestant work ethic of postwar America, Larry rejects all his friends' efforts to find him employment or help him in any way. He needs, not only a route out of his past, but also a new way of working; he needs, as he says unironically, to loaf.

As I read this book, considering Larry's travels and spiritual exercises against the backdrop of the Great Depression and the various catastrophes in his more conventional friends' lives, I began to make a conscious connection for the first time between physical and spiritual traveling. Larry Darrell traveled because he could not be at home in himself; in traveling he remade himself, and found a home. His nascent wisdom could even heal others. I was not sophisticated enough to understand the misogyny in Maugham's book, but I saw well enough that what Wilde offered me was a world beyond the provincial realm of my religion. It was possible to think, to travel, to take risks, to love one's own body and other bodies, and still gain spiritual insight. As Wilde and I discussed this book in class, I realized that he saw this as well: he and

I were very much on the same wavelength. Wilde began to show me a more integrated world of spirit and body than I had ever seen before.

Our dialogue along these lines continued through the winter. But Wilde had a dark ace up his sleeve. One day in April he handed out a typed work of moderate length by Aristotle, mimeographed on soothing blue paper. The title was simply *Poetics*; the essay itself was a puzzle. Beyond matters of plot and character, I had not thought much about the structure of plays, and Aristotle's essay centered on structure. To be a tragedy, he argued, a play had to meet a number of what struck me as rather intricate requirements. As I read through the essay, however, I found myself bumping up against a more ominous question: what was a tragedy? And why would anyone choose to write one? As far as I was concerned, tragedies occurred daily in the most ordinary places—the highway, the back yard, the town pool. When the television news broadcast reports of these events, I changed the channel. Tragedy was, to my way of thinking, a denial of God's truth for humankind. It was exactly the kind of error I had been trained to identify and resist in Sunday school. Now it stared me in the face.

Aristotle made claims for drama that seemed as foreign to me as his original Greek would have been. A tragedy, he argued, was "the imitation of an action that is serious . . . in a dramatic, not a narrative form; with incidents arousing pity and fear, wherewith to accomplish its catharsis of such emotions." In Christian Science we did not acknowledge the reality of pity and fear; in this essay Aristotle not only acknowledged their reality, but insisted that the audience experience them as part of the drama. A tragedy also involved a "Discovery," a change from ignorance to knowledge. This discovery did not interrupt or prevent the dramatic crisis, but led directly to it. Moreover, because pity and fear were the essential effects of tragedy, the tragic hero had to come upon his fate through "undeserved misfortune." It was essential, according to Aristotle, that the tragic hero's fortunes not shift from misery to happiness, "but on the contrary from happiness to misery; and the cause of it must lie not in any depravity, but in some great error on his part."

Throughout class that day, despite my admiration for Wilde, I found myself repeating the Scientific Statement of Being. "There is no life, truth, intelligence, or substance in matter," I reassured myself. The spiritual motion of life was from misery to happiness, not happiness to misery; in God's kingdom there was no misfortune. The Aristotelian essay before me was nothing more than a manifestation of mortal mind at play in its own unreal fields. I could study it, remember it, and use it for literary analysis, but I did not have to accept it or believe it.

And yet, trying to keep it at arm's length, I found passages coming back to mind, vying with Mary Baker Eddy's words for my attention. Wasn't it true that life moved from happiness to misery? Wasn't that, indeed, the story of Christ on the cross? "My God, My God, why has thou forsaken me?" I understood the other interpretations of this passage, of course, yet the plain reality of what Aristotle called a "Peripety"—the change from one condition to its opposite—refused to leave my mind. The consequence of this meditation was deeply troubling. Why encourage pity and fear, I wondered? What could be the use of tolerating a change from happiness to misery?

I thought of suicide at this point in a somewhat idle, abstract way, but the thought became more insistent as I read the next assignment, Sophocles' Oedipus Rex. In this play all of Aristotle's tragic formulae came terrifyingly to life. Oedipus, a good man whose only flaw is his quick temper, winds up fulfilling the grim fate prophesied for him. He is not depraved, nor does he seem to deserve this fate; its intensity and horror lie beyond his control. Having learned that he has slain his father and married his mother, he vows no longer to behold the ugliness of the suffering he has caused, and stabs out his eyes.

I first read this play in early May of 1972, on a lounge chair in the sunny backyard of my parents' house in Los Altos, where Bing cherries were ripening on the tree and the bees buzzed loudly among the roses. It was a paradisal setting, yet I had brought into it a serpent. "I would not have come to shed my father's blood," cried Oedipus, "nor been called among men the spouse of her from whom I sprang. But now I am forsaken of the gods . . . and if there is yet a woe sur- passing woes, it has become the portion of Oedipus." Those words fell upon my beautiful refuge like a monolithic shadow. What I held in my hands was, simply, the authority of evil. I had never before faced it in such irrefutable terms.

I did not think of the terms as being irrefutable then. On the contrary, I kept trying to refute them with all the prayerful rhetoric of my religion. But the old words of divine praise and spiritual argument fell dully against the intensity of the suffering of Oedipus. What Oedipus knew, I saw, was the unjustifiable excess of his punishment. The knowledge he acquired demanded not denial but an intense and articulate mourning of all that he had been or might have become. I was struck as if by a fist by his self-mutilation; it was at once too gruesome and too symbolic. Why not be done with it, I asked myself? Why not die?

In the sweetly fragrant backyard, I stared past the cherries and the roses, past the orange tree and the plum tree with its abundant crop. I felt as if life were being taken from me, as if my blood and breath had somehow become less real, less necessary. The rest of that day is lost to memory: I moved automatically through dinner and conversation, watched tele- vision, got undressed, went to bed. The next day I had a talk with Wilde.

It was clear from the outset of our discussion that Wilde could not fix what I wanted fixed: he could not reconcile tragedy with Christian Science. Yet I persisted.

"What good can come out of reading this?" I asked. "There is no good here at all." I was not so much angry as baffled. I wanted to believe I could be contradicted.

Wilde smiled slightly. "You're right," he said. "There is no good here. This is an ugly, horrible play about a very bad thing that happens to someone who doesn't deserve it. There is no reason for Oedipus's fate."

"But then why put up with it?" I demanded. "Why not reject fate? Why not appeal to a higher reality?"

Wilde looked at me with the hard gaze of a man with an exact answer, yet said nothing. Without invoking my religion, I tried to explain my view of a higher reality. He listened for a few minutes.

"*You* may be able to reject fate," he said finally. "Most people don't believe it's possible. The idea is not to escape or deny what befalls you. The idea is to face it, accept it, and choose."

I waited; he remained silent.

"Choose what?" I asked.

"Dignity," he said. "Tragedy is about human dignity. What Oedipus does after his discovery affirms his power to feel and respond. He is dignified. He chooses this. Look." Wilde opened *Oedipus Rex* to a scene near the end, and read Oedipus's lines in his passionate voice: " 'Apollo, friends, Apollo was he that brought these woes of mine to pass, these sore, sore woes; but the hand that struck the eyes was none save mine, wretched that I am! Why was I to see when light could show me nothing sweet?' "

I was struggling. "How can it be dignified to stab out your eyes? How can it be dignified to accept that you've done something terrible? How can it be dignified not to demand happiness?"

Wilde looked at me as if we had known each other since childhood. "Because that is what it means to be human," he said. After a moment of silence, I offered some fumbling words of departure, and left.

It seemed impossible for me to bring tragedy under the shelter of the pillar of cloud that had brought me to California. Given my intensified interest in Christian Science—I was even a member of the Sunday school steering committee in my local church—I ought to have rejected Wilde's view of the world. But I did not. I could not reject the honest curiosity of Aristotle or the passionate judgments of Oedipus; these were somehow too authentic to suffer the attenuations of my fumbling dogmatism.

It may also have been that I refused to reject them because of something that had trammeled my mind for two months— an event intimately connected with my life in the church. One Sunday afternoon in March, my parents left with five other couples from the congregation for a fly-in picnic in the Central Valley. Although my father was no longer a pilot, three other church members were; they owned or leased their own small planes. My father and mother rode along in one plane. The passengers in one of the other planes were the pilot's wife and the Sunday school superintendent, Mildred Valentine, and her husband.

My parents had told me they'd be gone until early evening. They did not get home until quite a bit later. I was not worried; I had my writing and artwork to do, and I went out for a while to play with friends. Around dinnertime I popped a frozen pizza in the oven and, when it was done, sat down to eat in front of the television. I'd had quite a fine day when they walked through the door, looking pale and subdued.

"How was it?" I asked, not really listening.

"It was OK," my father said.

"Tiring," my mother said. They went into the bedroom; I did not see them until morning, when they seemed more or less themselves.

That afternoon, when I opened the *Palo Alto Times,* I found a front-page story on the crash of a small airplane. Because the headline mentioned two Los Altos couples, I read on. I read more and more slowly as I got to the names—including Mr. and Mrs. Valentine's—and realized what had happened. According to the report, their plane had come in too high and too fast, stalled on an attempted go-around, and crashed into trees. The four occupants had been killed instantly.

My mother was reading in her bedroom. I went in and laid the paper on her lap. Then I went out.

Later, of course, my parents tried to explain everything to me, including their reasons for saying nothing when they got home. It all sounded very rational to me. It sounded rational to me, too, in a way, when the next Sunday our teacher explained to us that we couldn't judge Christian Science by Christian Scientists; we had to judge the religion by its principles. It was "a tragedy"—I wonder what Wilde would have thought of the Sunday school teacher's words—that Mr. and Mrs. Valentine had "passed on," but we could not judge our religion by their demise. Whatever individual failings appeared to occur in Christian Scientists' lives, the principle of the religion was unfailing and perfect. We should not, therefore, assume that the Valentines represented any weakness in the religion. The religion was without flaw, and we could take comfort in that fact.

Of course there was a certain rationality to all: a religion based on a scientific relationship between God and humankind must insist on the primacy of the principles behind that science, even when men and women suffer and die. Perhaps I was reassured to know that despite Mr. and Mrs. Valentine's deaths on impact, there was still no "life, truth, intelligence, or substance in matter." All was still "infinite Mind, and its infinite manifestation," as Mary Baker Eddy had written, "for God is All-in-all."

Yet the part of me that did not need to take comfort—that did not need to believe desperately in this religion—was revolted. This incident had been riddled with falsehoods. My parents could not tell me about it because they were afraid it would shake my religious faith; I had to find out from the newspaper, like any stranger. Later, as I reflected on what had occurred, I realized that they could not tell me because it was simply too horrible. They could not even really admit it to themselves, because they had only the language of "the real and eternal." Their own silent suffering must have been enormous. Like them, my Sunday school teacher could not admit the reality of these deaths; he too was afraid it would shake our faith, and thus seemed to blame the Valentines for their fate.

At all costs, the religion had to be preserved. Enormous human energy went into hanging up happy bunting around Christian Science that week, while friends laid wreaths on the Valentines' graves. I saw this; I was not stupid. But the culture of Christian Science was so deeply ingrained in me that I could not turn away. I continued to hope that if I remained faithful, I would move beyond the inconsistencies and find a place where both human beings and Christian Science were cherished.

This was not to happen. The accident hovered around me like a pliant lie, cooperative but inescapable. When I came, finally, to Oedipus, his deed demanded from me a response I could not easily give. To gain dignity was to acknowledge human limits—limits to the body, limits to knowledge—and to define oneself in terms of those limits. In tragedy that visceral knowledge of limits also became a form of love. Was it right, I wondered, to say that Oedipus ultimately loved himself? It seemed impossible, yet in his moment of authentic self-knowledge he took his life in hand with what I could only describe as a self-love devoid of egotism. It was a strange paradox, one that made no real sense to me. But it would not leave my mind. Oedipus's self-regard and courage seemed alien to the denial of death that enshrouded me.

Wilde assigned us other tragedies or variants of tragedy after *Oedipus Rex,* including Shakespeare's *Julius Caesar* and Hemingway's *The Old Man and the Sea.* But it was *Julius Caesar* that caught my imagination. Perhaps purely idiosyncratic pleasures drew me into the play—Cassius was "lean and hungry," as I was—or perhaps it was the brilliance of Mark Anthony's rhetoric. Beyond these possibilities lay the fact that Wilde chose the play for his final examination, terrifying us with the prospect of failure. We would face a series of quotations, he explained—some of them no more than three words long—and we would have to identify the scene, the speaker, and the context, and then explain the significance of the quotation to the play as a whole.

By this time I adored Wilde, although he called into question all that I had been raised to believe, and I had no intention of faltering on his exam. Thus I memorized the entire play. I did well on the exam, but that was not the greatest benefit. The night before the test, I dreamed the entire play—every character, every scene—with what my unconscious must have decided were authentic costumes and sets. I knew myself to be the only audience, caught up in delight at the danger and subterfuge and the precision of the language. When I awoke, it was as if I had just left Rome and all my friends were slowly fading in their tragic demise. I had lived a work of literature; I had gained from it an intensity of feeling that required no rationale, justification, or principle. For a brief time, liberated from my past, I lived another life. But no one escapes the past for long.

It may seem ironic that what I most remember about Wilde was his joy. Given his attire and his demeanor, not to mention his minute attention to the details of tragedy, I ought to remember him as a grim fellow, optimistic about knowledge but pessimistic about his students' chances of using it wisely. But this would render Wilde a stereotype—the mere opposite of the wise teacher I accepted a priori in Christian Science. Such a stereotype could not possibly be true. Wilde was a wise teacher not because he declared the unreality of evil—as I had been taught to do in Sunday school—but precisely because he declared its reality.

In acknowledging evil's power, Wilde brought it out from the shadows, where it had hidden in my experience under a variety of euphemisms—"error," "mental malpractice," "animal magnetism." In some ways, then, he made evil less frightening than Christian Science did. In Christian Science, evil was nothing, but it was a potentially powerful illusion. I knew firsthand how devastating those "illusions" could be, and yet I could not pin them down or direct my anger at them; praying against error in Christian Science became a form of shadow boxing, in which the shadow grew more ominous the more I was unable to hit it. For Wilde, however, evil was as real as the events that befell Oedipus. He named it; he asked us to choose and shape our lives in response to it. Thus he conferred upon us a sense of power which, though not without its terrors, more often than not led to joy.

I do not mean to confuse joy with happiness; it is possible to be suddenly joyous in the midst of great misery, or to know joy in the moments between misfortune. It is not possible to know happiness that way. Those of us in Wilde's class who became close friends had enough misery to go around, but this did not place joy beyond our reach. On the contrary, it may have been Wilde's teaching that gave us a way of articulating our common experiences.

It was in Wilde's class, for example, that I sealed my friendship with Jennie, a rather distant, brilliant girl who owned a sharpshooter's rifle, belonged to a drum and bugle corps, and used her ping-pong table at home as a staging ground for battles from the Revolutionary War, the Civil War, and assorted Napoleonic wars. I used to annoy her at chess because I played by instinct, using openings she had never seen. She always beat me, but it took her a while to realize that I did not know what I was doing. Her exasperation ultimately would bring out her sense of humor, which was quite lovely and which few people saw; we would laugh over my idiocy and her reaction.

In that moment of joy I felt at home, as I usually did in her household. The house was a fine old clapboard castle; its rooms could have been models for the many-chambered mansion of a rather eccentric deity. Jennie's room was upstairs, not far from the black iron fire escape that spiraled downward to the backyard. She occupied the top floor with her three brothers, Brady, Stephen, and Roy, and her parents. The rest of the house was given over to serious pursuits—reading, writing, experimenting, war games.

On occasion, after my desperate attempts at chess, Jennie and I would go see what her brothers were doing. Stephen was almost always a good choice. He might, for example, be attempting to launch his own Polaris missile. This involved a model rocket, some clever wiring, and a trash can filled with water. The rocket never made it out of the trash can, although the can made some fine shrapnel when it blew apart. Having ducked, we shook hands and congratulated ourselves on witnessing the event without coming to harm. It was virtually a success, since failure analysis was almost as interesting as a launch.

Jennie and I might also wander over to the ping-pong table, where over the course of several days she had arranged a Napoleonic battle according to one of her books on military history. The placement of troops, cannon, and headquarters was precise, with an elegance that knowledge always acquires in the aftermath of a disaster. The cannon actually fired small cannonballs—a detail of considerable pride for Jennie, which I misunderstood as an invitation to shoot. By the time Jennie realized what I was doing, I had wiped out half a regiment on the other side of the river. Characteristically, she refused to let me help her set them up again.

Although I seemed impulsive and undisciplined, and Jennie seemed the opposite, we actually shared a good many of each other's traits. Jennie's willingness to take risks constantly surprised me, and my own ability to strike to the heart of some vexing problem occasionally won her admiration. Somehow our lives had demanded that we show different strengths to the world, but with each other we were more aligned than we ever really cared to admit. We thus became friends and comrades.

Were we beautiful bodies? That notion, which I had learned in Pennsylvania as part of my need for love, became a question for the first time with Jennie; it had an element of danger which I had never felt before. As we lay around her living room reading "Star Trek" novels, I would look over at her from time to time and see in her perfect ease a source of desire. But my desire was different, and more insistent, than my childhood desire for Laura or Leslie. With this new desire I remained even more myself; the more I desired, the less I imagined myself as one with Jennie. There was no easy combination of transcendence and immanence, which had characterized my childhood passions although I did not know the words for that experience.

At the prep school in Pennsylvania I had had a Bible class which turned out to be a catchall for whatever the school felt the students needed to know about surviving. Though they never taught what I most needed to know, they happened to use this class for sex education. We had a textbook, with line drawings of pubescent bodies and genitalia, and a series of chapters which discussed sexual behavior in a way that struck me as being both sketchy and condescending. When the teacher said at one point, "I don't doubt that some of you in this room right now are capable of producing children," we were unimpressed. I emerged from that class as I ultimately emerged from the school as a whole—miserable and sick, with my mind on other things.

Because the subject of passion never came up in that class— how could it have come up?—I had never really made a connection between sexuality, desire, and the deep sources of one's selfhood. My source of selfhood remained rooted in Christian Science, despite tremors of doubt; my so-called body remained a metaphor for the spiritual ideas of reliability, precision, grace, and happiness. What, then, was this feeling that seemed to make me a different creature? What came over me to make me feel even more like myself and yet somehow distant from the girl who lay a few feet away from me on the couch, reading about tribbles? I did not want to explain it to myself, and so did not. Yet it seemed related, somehow, to tragedy: it was not to be wished away, or translated into spiritual terms. It was sexual, serious, and ineradicable.

It was also susceptible to sublimation, at least in its early stages. Passion sprang from more than one source, and although sexual passion frightened me I was perfectly capable of responding to political and romantic passion. Jennie became the catalyst for these responses. Her intelligence and independence made her impatient with some of the more rigidly bureaucratic features of high school, especially the required physical education classes. Even at that time she was serious about her body—she would later row at Yale and Oxford, then take up bicycle racing—and she suffered from the sexual prejudices inherent in high school P.E. She wanted to play football and baseball and soccer with the boys, or to develop her own routine of running, weight training, and bicycling. Instead she was required to play rudimentary forms of field hockey and volleyball with the other girls, who on the whole were not particularly interested. She did not like them because they were not serious; they hated her because they felt that she intimidated them. When, during a hockey game, one of the girls swung her stick like a golf club and hit Jennie in the chest, Jennie called a foul and was promptly thrown out; the teacher, who was also the referee, worried that Jennie might hurt the other girl. The incident thus became Jennie's fault, a judgment which only added to her conviction that she was misunderstood. Her sense of hurt and confusion at the end of that day was as great as any I had ever seen. She was later removed from P.E. and permitted to pursue her own athletic interests, not because her teacher saw the merit in her proposal, but because—in the teacher's words—Jennie was unfit for team sports.

At first I found this a source of intellectual outrage. I talked to her about it, and wrote a paper for Wilde on the dark ability of conformists to misunderstand the motives of the non-conformist. Then the unnamable passion arose again in me, and under its influence I wrote my first poem. It was a love poem, though I tried to conceal that fact; it was addressed to Jennie, though it never named her. In a typical double message, I offered the poem to her for consolation but did not tell her until several years later that she was the *you* of the poem. Of course she had figured it out rather quickly.

I had thus written a poem for a girl whose alienation from conventional life seemed as vivid as her own idiosyncratic talents. I wanted to heal her misery, but found Christian Science too tame for that mission. Poetry was better— stronger. Through it I could preserve my own voice, invoke my own deities. It was an iconoclastic decision which, like many such decisions, I made without reflection or anxiety. It was simply necessary.

For me the beauty of poetry was inseparable from the beauty of bodies, yet it had one essential advantage: it did not require contact with beautiful bodies. It required contact instead with words, sounds, methods, ideas, music. It was sensuous without being sensual. Thus it bought me time as I wrestled with passions that drew me more and more ardently to bodies themselves—to their fragrances, their caresses, their private and fundamental responses to love. I did not see myself as walking a tightrope between Christian Science and sexuality, but of course I was. Poetry was my balancing pole. In words I could give a sublimated shape and context to my passions; I could engage the spirituality of my religion without abandoning the intensity of my life in the world. This approach worked for several years—well beyond my senior year in high school—until the real lesson of Oedipus came home to me, and I too wanted to destroy my sight out of misery for what I saw. Then, in a new incarnation, poetry once again came to my rescue. But it came with all the hardness and misery that Wilde knew he had somehow to teach us.

THE PAST IS A BATTLEFIELD STREWN WITH MINES WHOSE DETonators finally fail: in the end, the oldest miseries no longer explode. Like mines, ominous and encrusted with dirt, they look threatening, but when shaken or dropped after excavation they do not detonate. They lie there, frozen in their treachery, incapable of harm.

My unrelieved earaches, which were such a torment to me in my childhood, no longer wound me in the gut. I hold them in my mind as I would hold a mine, delicately and cautiously, and then I let them fall. Nothing happens. At most they displace a little dust. I am outraged at what I endured, but it rarely frightens me. I am only frightened when I see such torments inflicted in the present on children who unlike me do not live through the battle. My old memories of earaches, bronchitis, and unnamed and unhealed illnesses return with a keen edge, a sharp fear of human beings who impose suffering for the sake of a principle. But the fear is short-lived. I have learned to move beyond it into a healthy rage.

Other mines, still relatively fresh, have live detonators. Buried in my personal battlefield of high school and college, they remind me how much there is to mourn. I was living a dream in Christian Science. It was a beautiful dream. It rejected everything that frightened me about life; it promised comfort and healing if only I would turn away from beautiful bodies and their consequences. But I could not turn away. I was drawn to bodies as Oedipus was drawn to knowledge, sensing the dangers he might unearth.

Although the religious shield around me was fallible, it was nevertheless comforting. When, a few months after Wilde's class, I began to date, I still could somehow rationalize my passion as a spiritual desire: what I wanted was not to make bodily love, but to experience the spiritual unity that transcended body. It happened, rather coincidentally, that this spiritual unity began with the body—began with a brief, tentative kiss outside the home of my first girlfriend Janet on a moonless California night—but that was essentially an illusion, a metaphor for the real love in the process of creating itself.

It seems strange, now, to realize how nearly right I was— and how desperately wrong. I was right that love is not preexistent; human beings are perpetually creating it. They do so, however, not through any airy thinness of mingled souls, but through the exacting presence of bodies. Neither unreal nor unwilling, our bodies nevertheless make their own demands. They are fundamental and cannot be abstracted. At the time, however, I hoped ardently that my abstractions would outlast the kiss.

To acknowledge sexual pleasure was to admit the reality of the unreal; I could not see myself as having permission to do this. Yet, when I sat on the lawn outside the school with Janet, talking of books and summer plans, I could not disentangle our conversation from the sight of her summer dress opening a little as she lay facing me on the lawn, arousing a desire for an intimacy I could not know with the mind alone.

Heavily sublimated, my desire for Janet took on an authoritarian cast: I wanted to be around her all the time, to be her one boyfriend, to earn her undying devotion. She was too wise for me. When I waited for her at every recess, ate every lunch with her, and planned my life around her, she heard the voice of doom. In the privacy of her room she announced our breakup with a gentle elegance I later came to admire; at the time I was crushed. How had I deserved such rejection? For a month I mourned, unable to make use of a practitioner's advice that the best relationships between boys and girls were not too deep. Then I noticed a new presence on the school lawn—a girl who often wore a short leather skirt and a straw sun hat, who tied her hair back in a thick braid and startled me with her fierce gaze. For several days I walked past her, always trying to catch her eye, always turning away abruptly when she looked, stricken by the intensity of her smile. Then, in a blast of courage, I introduced myself. Her name, she said, was Lesley.

Because she was a year younger than I, we had no classes together, and I could not bring myself to eat lunch with her on the lawn. For a couple of weeks I would eat lunch quickly by myself, then just happen to pass the lawn on the way to somewhere else. She would be there; we would talk for a few minutes about Warren Wilde, whom she had as a teacher, or

about her readings in Wilde's class, or about how hard it was
to master the Cyrillic alphabet in her Russian class. She
seemed to be waiting for something—for me to sit down and
have lunch with her, at least—but, still shy from my earlier
romantic experience, I was reluctant.

Things might have stalled out permanently if it had not
been for the *Troubadour,* the student literary magazine for
which Wilde served as the faculty advisor. I had joined the
staff the previous year; Lesley made an appearance as a new
member. Arriving a little late at the first meeting of the season,
joking with the other staff members I knew well, I caught
sight of Lesley at the end of the table and stumbled slightly
over my greeting. After a couple of hours of reading and
discussing manuscripts, we brought the meeting to a close,
and people began to drift out. Lesley got up to gather her
books, which she had left on a table near her violin case. At
the outset Lesley's violin attracted me almost as much as she
did. I had never actually held a violin, although I played the
guitar and was partial to Bach and Rachmaninov. The violin
seemed itself a work of art, a gorgeous instrument of mystery.
I had to say something. Lesley and I spoke to each other with
comical deference.

"Would it be possible for me to see your violin?" I asked.

"I don't usually let anyone else touch it," she said with a
beautiful pause. "But I guess it's alright."

Holding the violin, admiring its luminous finish and del-
icate shaping, I thought I had in my hands the spiritual ideal
of music. But I also knew I was holding a beautiful instrument
which belonged to a woman who loved music and poetry,
and who had just broken one of her own private rules for
me. The violin gave me a way of talking to her while I tried
to figure out what I really wanted to say.

Because we saw each other regularly at the magazine meet-
ings, the pressure on us eased: I did not have to invent excuses
to talk to her. Nor did I need to invent fantasies about her.
I was present in the midst of her reality—her keen analysis
of poems and stories, her indignant religious arguments, her

frustration, her sense of humor, her laughter. To work with her on the magazine was to talk and argue and joke with a genial companion; at times I almost, almost forgot that I was falling in love with her. It was a long descent, infinitely pleasant, as the year wound down and we found ourselves sitting next to each other at the last performance of the school play, *A Midsummer Night's Dream*.

The luxury of these days was so great that I almost forgot what the end of school might mean: suddenly we would no longer be thrown together. Warming up to each other slowly, saying little about our feelings and enjoying the ambiguous ground between friendship and passion, we had forgotten that at some point we would have to declare our intentions. I could not anticipate Lesley's desires, but about my own I was confused. I wanted her badly, yet I had an inkling of what that might mean—how far it might go, how far it might pull me from my quest for spiritual love. Would I say good-bye to her then, at the end of the summer, as my practitioner suggested?

Lesley belonged to the American Field Service club on campus, which sponsored international students at the high school and celebrated the end of each year with a beach picnic. She invited me; I accepted. The picnic took place on a beautiful stretch of sand about forty-five miles south of San Francisco. In the wispy fog we set up a volleyball net, got a fire going, and boiled water for fresh clams. I hated clams, but the day was beautiful in a classic California genre, and I loved being around Lesley.

We played on the same team, missing digs and spiking the ball repeatedly into the Pacific; we played on opposite teams, competing as though we were the only two people playing. After a couple of hours, however, I tired of volleyball, small talk, and coyness. Since the beach was long I set out on a walk. Before I left, I glanced back at Lesley on the off chance that she might have noticed my departure. She was laughing happily with someone else.

Five minutes of walking carried me well down the beach, toward the high cliffs and caves I loved to explore. The ocean thundered beside me, wrapping me in its harsh modulations, taking me out of my humanity. I felt relieved. But when I heard, through the sound of the ocean, the sharper sound of a runner's feet on sand, I turned around with a hope I dared not feel. In the second before Lesley reached me, as we locked gazes, I saw in her eyes the intensity of my own love, my own desire. Slowing but not stopping, she caught me in a reckless embrace that spun us around on the sand.

As we waded into the surf, holding each other against the intensity of the waves, we had no words for love. We needed the language of an embrace, of bodies against the surf, of two wet and cold people laughing at their folly. A half-hour later, when we walked back to the party, we spoke the casual words of old friends. The ocean was our backdrop, its irregular rhythm a source of comfort as we discussed our musical training and our memories of the first rhythms we had ever really noticed—the waves, the beating of our hearts.

Yet as the summer progressed we found that our words did not quite mesh. Or perhaps they meshed too well: we sounded too much like copies of one another, people so much on the same wavelength that their match must have been made in heaven. We liked Arthur Miller and Samuel Beckett, Corelli and Barber; we showed each other our poems, we played music together. When we simply hung around during the long, sunny California evenings, talking about whatever came to mind, it seemed as if our time together could never end. Yet we were both somehow dissatisfied. Taking a superficial pleasure in our perfect match, we shielded our differences from each other. I talked little about Christian Science; she talked little about her unorthodox faith in a unifying spirit of nature and humankind. When these matters began to emerge, we distracted ourselves for the time being with happier subjects. With each act of muting, however, we chafed against our own private realities. We began to argue.

When I insisted on trying to explain Christian Science to her, she pointed out its apparent logical fallacies with a keenness which infuriated me. We grew defiant with each other for the sake of defiance.

When we finally broke up, toward the end of that summer, there was no mourning on either side. I was writing a short book on T. S. Eliot's poems, and threw myself into the remainder of the project with all the passion I had reserved for a different love. Jennie and I spent more time together; she and I typed the final version of my manuscript, setting up two typewriters on a single table and stopping from time to time to talk about the injustices of life. In the end it seemed like a fine summer. I did not miss Lesley much.

Except that, of course, I did. I had thought I disliked Lesley's form of intellectual combat, but in fact disagreeing with her was refreshing, even liberating. She mastered both an intellectual and a physical directness: in her they seemed to spring from the same source, so that I felt in her kisses or embraces the same kind of passion she applied to her ideas and arguments. She was very beautiful; her absence left a sullen breeze floating through my life. I could rationalize this as an opportunity for me to clear the air with a renewed devotion to Christian Science, yet as I studied *Science and Health* and read the Bible I kept drifting back to moments with Lesley—long talks on our walks in the coastal range, a frank discussion of the liabilities of love in light of her parents' divorce—until I wearied of the competing claims on my mind, and set my religion aside for awhile.

Lesley and I stayed apart for several months, seeing other friends, not really dating but certainly not hibernating, until one evening in late October of my senior year. As a rather clumsy yearbook editor, I found myself putting in long hours at school, laying out pages and cropping photographs; Lesley was officiating at a fund-raising dinner for the AFS club. When I finished my work, I wandered over to the cafeteria to see how the dinner was going. A large crowd had gathered, and I spent a couple of hours with Lesley and other friends.

I had planned to stay only a few minutes, yet as Lesley and I talked it was as if our old hostilities had bred a kind of magic. We were real to each other in a way we had not been in the summer. The change was delicious, tantalizing. I stayed long into the evening, helping Lesley clean up the tables and prepare the cafeteria for the morning rush. Then I offered to drive her home. On the way we stopped at my house, and in the unhurried expanse of late evening we began to find an intimacy beyond words.

Never had I felt so loved; never had I felt so whole. In our time together there was no mind-body split, but a unity that granted us a brief, oblivious peace. Happy together, we grew increasingly close as the year progressed. Yet, as our intimacies became more elaborate, I began to hear a dark voice of authority: was I not, in fact, glorifying the body, the unreal anti-fact of life? Mary Baker Eddy was quite explicit that sex was a concession to the illusion of human existence, and should "only be permitted for the purpose of generating"; what, then, did I think I was doing?

In fact, I had already decided at some level that sexual pleasure could not be avoided without abstracting my passion, and thus making it a kind of lie. The question of abstinence seemed contrived or artificial to me: it was a dividing line with no relevance to my own experience. Nevertheless, I felt progressively farther from God as I moved closer to the one aspect of my life that seemed truly real to me. The pathos of these occasions was almost comical: utterly at peace in my love one moment, I would be wracked with guilt the next, wondering if my adventures in "unreality" would somehow yield horrible illusions, nightmarish results. And then, seeking to appease unappeasable forces, I would simply try to deny intellectually the reality of my passion.

I made several attempts to discuss these anxieties with Christian Science practitioners, but always ran hard against their placid lives: they could not discuss sexuality. The subject of birth control was of course out of the question. Even condoms, which I had once inspected curiously as a child on a

New Jersey beach, now gave too much credence to the reality
of my experience, and so Lesley and I lived in terror of accidental pregnancy. Finally revolted with my own idiocy, I
made the obligatory trip to the drug store and effectively
knocked the foundations out from under my religious faith.

I now see the utter ordinariness of this ordeal. How many
teenagers with strong religious convictions fall prey to the
same "temptations"? It is ludicrous that people should suffer
so when so much knowledge is available to them. This kind
of judgment, however, in no way lessens the terror that a
deeply religious teenager will feel when passion ignites. The
question is not simply a matter of sexuality, but a matter of
identity. The teenager must choose what part of himself or
herself to keep and what part to mourn. That I was entirely
unprepared to do this is at once a great tribute to my religion
and a great indictment.

In certain ways I was quite innocent—innocent particularly
of the process of mourning, in which one lays pieces of oneself
and one's faith to rest when they can no longer serve. I had
no tolerance for mourning: I would let go of nothing. I would
keep my religion, my sexuality, my selfhood, my innocence;
I would not choose.

These memories, though nearly seventeen years old, still
have the capacity to detonate. Automatically, from years of
training, I chastise myself even now for loving bodies, remembering that I should love the "real and eternal, not the
unreal and temporal." A wave of guilt, of conflicting allegiances, washes over me: is this the explosion? No—I have
come too far, I think, for the old faith to harm me. Yet I
have not defused it; I have not entirely separated its falsehoods
from its truths. For I do believe that Christian Science contains
certain truths of divine love. I also believe that conventions
of doctrine and culture have made those truths highly inac-
cessible. Perhaps this is the view of all apostates. Yet to escape
the worst influences of any religion—to choose one's own
faith, rather than the faith that is chosen for one—is to disarm
the religion, to remove its detonator. In this case the detonator

might seem to be a kind of extremist spirituality, but it is also a turgid mass of emotional responses: guilt and shame, a paranoid fear of being outside of God's universe and God's care, a horror of meaninglessness, a sense of life amounting to nothing.

This is where I began, with the fear of nothingness. It seems strange that in that beginning I gave this story a rather literary cast, as if the course of such a meditation were not to escape but rather to write about the escape—to create a diversion for readers. Perhaps that was a form of self-protection, an unstated promise that, whatever I wrote, I would never bring this book too close to a raw nerve. But the nerves are showing now.

The question of nothingness or meaninglessness is not literary: it has its roots, in this case, in my response to the choice I finally had to make between my religion and what I perceived to be real. In this choice I faced the reality of death—my own, and the deaths of my family and friends—for the first time. I could not dispel this reality; I could not call on my faith to dispel it; I could not apologize for my judgment that Christian Science seemed finally too limited to cope adequately with death. Thus part of me died. But I would not let it die; I kept trying to summon it back from the grave, like Lazarus, too afraid of the new self that might emerge. The blankness that ensued, the sense of meaninglessness, has still not dispersed. But the sources of the pain are clearer.

In 1976, at the age of thirty-six, Warren Wilde died in a dentist's chair during minor periodontal surgery. He lived with many stresses, and his briefcase was always full of tranquillizers. His death was explained as a reaction to the combination of anesthesia and some tranquillizer he happened to use without informing the oral surgeon. It was the kind of end he had sometimes joked about—at once personal and a comment on the human experience, like Cyrano's death or Edgar Allan Poe's. I heard about his death at Stanford, and in the next few weeks I found him accompanying me on my long walks through the hills behind campus. His words were always the same—the ones he had written to me at the end of my sophomore year: "Keep forever your fresh and young sense of wonder and inquiry," he reminded me as I walked. "There are vast realms before you, capabilities to be explored and rendered articulate."

In those hills behind Stanford the near ridges hid the higher ones from view, but a vigorous walk could take me up to the highest ridge, where live oaks bent low to the ground in the harsh winds. As I climbed an oak, the whole of the Bay Area spread out before me, growing tiny as the earth itself grows tiny from a far distance. "Even the midnight world of Dostoyevsky," Wilde continued, "the blackbirds of Van Gogh, the wonders of Shakespeare, as Loren Eiseley has so cogently stated, are particle episodes that manifest the fact that man's world can never really be fully explored." Even then, years after having Wilde in class, I heard his electric and slightly grandiloquent voice. I listened to him, and mourned him, and wondered what I could choose to do in a diminished world.

6

GHOSTS

THE PERSON WHO PEERS OUT AT ME FROM THE ATTIC WIN-
dow looks familiar, but is hard to see. I cross the street
to the other sidewalk, hoping for a better angle of view. It
helps: I can make out the pale hair, and the glancing light
across the forehead must be from wire-rimmed glasses. Staring more intently, hoping to fix the person's gaze in mine,
I'm suddenly startled by the sound of footsteps. I turn—not
too abruptly. The man in the house behind me is taking out
the garbage. He eyes me but offers no greeting. When I glance
back at the window, I see only the smears of dirt and dust
that even now look a little like a face. Was no one there after
all? I walk on, a suspicious character.

Yet I might well have been in that window, I tell myself,
aware that I am nursing an illusion. Some illusions, like
ghosts, are useful for making sense of difficult transforma-
tions: we use them to explain ourselves to ourselves. I pass
by this house in Cambridge from time to time to see if that
is my ghost in the upper window. At one point in my life—

a still point, the eye of a hurricane—I occupied the upper room, paying my twenty-five dollars a week to two old sisters who ran the place as a rooming house for poor students, would-be writers, and a few people in a long free fall toward homelessness. The sisters must have died or moved away; the house now looks so different, with its new wooden shingles and salmon trim, that it could not possibly belong to the same people. Whoever the new owners are, they have almost redeemed this house from its past: I did not recognize it when I first came by, more than ten years after living here, to look for ghosts. I had to check the number to be sure.

Looking beyond the renovations, beyond the walls themselves, and into the past, I glide up the stairs to the second-floor kitchen, reserved for the tenants, where a young man is fixing bacon and eggs. It is early morning—earlier than the man usually rises. He does not like to get up at this hour; his room under the eaves is always cold, and in the stark September light he knows the day will last for a long, long time. It would be better, he tells himself, to go back to sleep, to sleep for hours, to awaken only when everyone else in the house has gone out. But some of the tenants, who work night shifts, get up at noon; others almost never go out. Someone is always in the kitchen, making a sandwich or reading a newspaper or simply smoking. Their lives seem tiny and frightening, and so the man rises early, before any of them, to make his breakfast in solitude.

The solitude keeps him going, because he has died but does not yet know whether he will remain in the tomb or come back from it. The tomb is quite large: this house is one room of it, and Harvard, where he has come to study, is another room, and his evening walks through Cambridge are yet another room. Does he know he is dead? That is not quite clear. Do the dead ever know that they are dead? Most of the time he moves mechanically, eating little and sleeping fitfully, reading Chaucer and Le Corbusier, avoiding other people. Every now and then, in odd places—Pusey library, the Red Line subway, the Fogg museum—he will sense a fit of despair coming on. It will arrive as it did when he was thirteen, with a wave of nausea, and he will have to leave quickly and walk until he is very tired. The despair suggests that he is not dead, but again this is not clear: it could be his punishment in the inferno.

Sometimes at night, when the clouds reflect the city lights in an aura around his room and he cannot sleep, he lies in bed, unsure of whether he is, and thinks back on when he was alive. He remembers how in the previous winter at Stanford, he discovered he could no longer feel God's love. When he read the words of *Science and Health* and the Bible, as he did devotedly, the words stayed words: they did not breathe life into his waning heart. The practitioners he talked to urged him to foresake his thoughts of bodies, to turn from his earlier sexual awakening; then he would feel God's love again. He listened listlessly, having already anticipated their advice.

Gradually words became his enemies. He could not seem to make them work. In his poetry class, he lost interest in reading and writing. His long walks in the hills behind Stanford yielded no new insights, no poems. Then the fits of despair began. He hated his body and its humanity; he prayed that it would be taken from him. He regretted every bodily thing he had ever done. His own sexuality repulsed him. Unable to concentrate or write at all, he dropped out of college. His parents sent him to another round of practitioners. He grew worse. It came to him one day that if he was not already dead, he would die soon.

As if by magic, a frightening reprieve came. He flew to England, where despite his continuing fits of despair he managed both to study and to vanish regularly into the woods around Cliveden. One day, staring into the eyes of a field-mouse, he thought he heard God's voice as his own voice. In its harsh way it comforted him. He knew then that he would not die. He also knew with equal force that he was not, exactly, alive. It was as if a vaporous, tactile fog had wrapped itself around him like a shroud, keeping him back for a time from the world. Too exhausted and frightened to choose, he accepted it.

In England he learned that he had been accepted to Harvard. He flew back to California briefly, at the end of the summer, where for a week he made repeated pilgrimages to the Palace of the Legion of Honor in San Francisco. He would sit on the bluffs overlooking the Golden Gate Bridge for hours, observing minute shifts in the afternoon mist. Then, seeing no other way, he boarded a flight for Boston and came to this rooming house, where the fog around him dispersed and he faced—not the warm light of day—but something paler and more austere, like a quantity of nothing in a dying body.

He stops remembering, then, as if he has gone as far with hateful words as he can. He reaches out for walls that are not there—rock walls, damp with underground seepage, tomb walls. The reaching seems to be an instinct; or perhaps it is his way of warding off something, of still trying to keep something at bay. This minor physical action triggers a flood of images: brown slopes covered with manzanita and laurel, secret terrains among the eucalyptus. But images hold no future. An image of a place, or even the place itself, cannot feed him or clothe him or give him another day. He might go to these places simply to be, but being, as he has been taught, is not enough: one must do, act, argue for divine truth. He has grown fatally tired of arguing.

He goes to the Grolier bookshop one day, at 6 Plympton Street, almost by accident. (The books for his course in Old English are sold out at the Harvard Coop, and he has heard a rumor that the Grolier might have one or two.) He does not know anything about the Grolier; he does not know that it sells only poetry. On this day the rain is a formidable monster, and the clasps on his ten-dollar fold-up raincoat have never really worked. He is quite wet and cold by the time he arrives.

Suppose you have come into the Grolier at the same moment as the storm-rattled young man; you notice him, but only because you are scanning the store itself, trying to get used to where you are. The Grolier is an old, one-room relic with high ceilings and shelves ten or twelve feet tall. A collection of tables in the middle of the room holds the new releases. One aisle, perhaps three feet wide at best, runs around the outer edge of the tables. Books rise up the walls like polychromy in a nineteenth-century American imitation of a cathedral.

You are, perhaps, looking for a biography of Hart Crane, which takes you up to the top of the ladder where the Cs are shelved. There, poised slightly above the rest of the world, you pause for a moment to look around. The proprietor stands by her desk in the far corner, figuring accounts. Another customer with a dark beard and a long black rain slicker studies the collection of Robert Lowell's work. Lowell died ten days ago in New York. The only other customer is the young man, whose cheap silvery raincoat is almost as horrible as his drenched deerstalker—never a cap for stormy weather. Dripping and shivering, he is a small storm in himself; you wonder if the proprietor will ask him to leave, or at least offer him a towel.

As long as he stays, however, he is interesting to watch. He has been staring at a volume just below your ladder for two or three minutes now. It seems to transfix him. When he finally reaches for it, he seems tentative. It is almost as if he cannot believe the book is real. Something about his exaggerated manner makes you worry about him. He looks up suddenly, instinctively sensitive to a long stare, and you wobble on the ladder: he has you. Unable to escape, you smile. He smiles oddly and turns away. You go back to watching.

The young man gathers up three books by Wendell Berry, then moves to the Fs, then to the Ms. You can see the major collections from where you stand—Robert Frost, John Milton, Marianne Moore, Thomas Merton—but the man chooses no books from among these. He did not seem to be looking for much of anything when he came in. Now, having laid his hat on a table and brushed his hair back, he suddenly seems intent, directed. He is choosing very carefully. When he is done, he hands over his small stack of books to the proprietor and looks at you. You are so startled by the difference in his face that you stare back for a moment, wondering if you have been watching the same man all along.

Did something happen, in those brief moments? You cannot remove from your mind the look he gave you before he left. His eyes might have been lasers, yet you thought you saw right through them. Uncanny. But how could you say to yourself that you saw a dead man emerging from the tomb?

IN CHRISTIAN SCIENCE A CENTRAL METAPHOR FOR HEALING IS light shining into darkness. Taking no cognizance of the darkness, the light simply and effectively obliterates it. Light, of course, is the metaphor for reality, darkness for unreality. The fact that, in the human world, both darkness and light are realities does not seem to most Christian Scientists to be a flaw in the analogy.

It is about 1:00 A.M., September 23, 1977. The cool evening darkness keeps a vigil at my window. It is steady, restful; I recall that it now stretches from here to California. I glance out into the darkness from the circle of light below my study lamp, where Wendell Berry's *Openings* lies open to "Grace":

> *The woods is shining this morning.*
> *Red, gold and green, the leaves*
> *lie on the ground, or fall,*
> *or hang full of light in the air still.*

This evening I have the light and the darkness. For the first time since I arrived here, the darkness does not frighten me. I do not expect the nightmares, the fits of shaking, the long wait for a long day. The darkness is restful. The page below me, like the woods in my mind, is full of light.

Perfect in its rise and in its fall, it takes
the place it has been coming to forever.
It has not hastened here, or lagged.

This woods, I see, is perfect, not by virtue of any a priori
concept of spiritual flawlessness, but by virtue of its integrity,
its wholeness. It rises and falls because that is what it does.
It grows at its own pace, not because that is the "right" pace
but because it is *its own*.

See how surely it has sought itself,
its roots passing lordly through the earth.
See how without confusion it is
all that it is, and how flawless
its grace is.

I have been graceless, flawed, full of confusion, bowed
down to a vision of life that has never allowed me to live in
the world. I have not been lordly.

Running or walking, the way
is the same. Be still. Be still.
"He moves your bones, and the way is clear."

"Running or walking, the way is the same." How long
have I been running, stumbling, falling face down on sharp
stones? There is no rush, this poem says, no haste, no end to
be achieved before anyone else: there is no competition, no
final prize, no winner. There is simply life, and the possibility
of wholeness that emerges within it. Before wholeness is the
inferno; at the advent of wholeness "the way is clear." Somehow, earlier today, as I dragged myself out of the downpour
into the bright room of the Grolier bookshop, I reached an
edge of the inferno: some ragbag of ideas and desires, long
subdued, gathered themselves into a critical mass and burst
through the bars of my prison cell. What I feel is the deep

restfulness of healing, yet the words are not from my religion. They are from the world.

Now even the smallest movements of my arms, my fingers, seem deliberate and elegant, as if illuminated from within. The circle of light around my book grows to include my own beautiful body. The darkness is a crescent underneath my skin. Between breaths, I hear someone speaking in a voice I can almost place. He has come into the room, a stranger drawn from the proud moments of my past, and asked me to arise. In rising, I see the room as it is: a bare place with pale blue wallpaper, a dark armchair, a bed, a narrow desk. I am alone. I look around for the stranger who has spoken to me, and find that he is I. The lamp glows on the dark desk. I take up the next book, Kenneth Fields's *Smoke,* and open to "North Point":

> *There is a going into deeper water*
> *Where there are no lights, no channels.*
>
> *The anonymous fog does not speak of stars.*
> *The drift and stop of buoys does not reach so far.*
>
> *Even if there were a compass, I would not want*
> *To look at it, its needle spinning crazily*
>
> *With me at the center waiting, still.*
> *I do not know if I could ever move*
>
> *Out to the point, trembling with all that I am not,*
> *Making my mind up, going where I go.*

These might be my own words. They are not, yet the fear is my fear, the sense of beauty my own. Yes, I say to myself, drawn again to the darkness beyond the window, at a certain point there is beauty even in fear: under the compression of a great weight, a burden of despair or tragedy, life reduces itself to the elemental fact of choice. In the last resort, we are neither predestined nor utterly abandoned, but emergent beings. How frightening it is to emerge—to leave behind the

old pain that has defined us! We might at least love our
weakness, as Jesus tenderly loved the weak and benighted.
We might embrace it like a wound, or some neurotic stig-
mata. But to leave it—to creep out to the point, enacting a
small, ineradicable courage—what does that do to us? Does
it make us unlovable? Does Jesus love the strong as well as
the weak?

He loves—I hear myself say, as if suddenly prompted—
the weak, and the ones who trust in fate to help them choose
their fate. I recall my first encounter with Kenneth Fields. By
the beginning of my junior year at Stanford, I had distinguished myself in a minor way as a literary scholar. I was
invited to join the English honors program, along with ten
or twelve other undergraduates. The honors program was a
form of accelerated life, as most of my schooling had been.
Those of us who were admitted understood that we were
identified as likely candidates for graduate study. Our reading
and seminar discussions would be close parallels to our probable experiences as graduate students, and would give us the
additional background in literature and theory needed to survive the intellectual jungle of graduate school.

I loathed the thought of the honors program. At the same
time, it seemed chosen for me: it was the logical culmination
of the work I had done at Stanford. I could not say no. Thus,
one afternoon, I walked down the corridor of the inner quad
toward Building 40, where I would turn in my letter accepting
admission to the program. At that moment—at that very
moment, as if a film director had suddenly rolled the camera
on his next scene—Kenneth Fields walked out the door. Although I had not met him before, I knew he taught the graduate poetry writing workshop. I had heard him read his
poems; I admired him greatly. Now I simply smiled at him
as I walked toward my fate.

He put out his hand to stop me. "You're Tom Simmons,
aren't you?" he asked. "Tim showed me some of your work."
(Timothy Dekin, an unknown poet with a dark, exceptional
talent, was one of my previous teachers.)

I held onto my letter for the honors program tightly, as if to keep it from crumpling.

"I have a spot open in the graduate writing workshop this term," Fields said to me. "You're welcome to have it."

I said what years of good behavior had trained me to say. "That's awfully nice," I replied, "but I'm about to join the honors program. Doesn't it meet at the same time as your class?"

Fields thought for a second. "Yes, it does," he said. "You're a good writer. Keep it in mind." The hand he'd held out to stop me now offered a wave of parting, and he was gone.

Even well-trained people cannot be stupid forever, especially when they detect the faint aroma of fateful choice. I watched him walk down the corridor, then ran after him.

"Professor Fields," I called. We stopped a good six feet from each other: it was a kind of face-off, with a no man's land of uncertainty and hope between us. "I'd like to join your workshop."

"Fine," he said. "See you tomorrow at 2:15 in the Jones Room." I crumpled my honors program letter into a tight ball.

That term with Fields went well; my poems, haphazard and clumsy, developed some trace of compression and subtlety under his direction. The next term, with a different, hostile professor, was part of the disaster that delivered me to misery. Now, months later, three thousand miles from Fields, I read his words and know that he embodied in a poem the experience I face. Despite my fear, I have to make some kind of choice.

My life has seemed a fiction, a fraud. What has brought me here? Trying to escape my own despair, hoping that if I only dedicated myself more fully to Christian Science I could recover my mind, I came to Harvard to become the scholar I would not be at Stanford. It was a futile gesture—almost a form of begging: just give me a quiet mind, I said to my past, and I will do whatever you want. I will excell again. I will demonstrate the rich, orderly presence of the divine Mind in my scholarship. But please, please rid me of these doubts and quandaries; above all rid me of any belief in the reality of the body.

My past insisted I was lying to myself. Out of that crucible of lies it propelled a hot core of possibilities—authentic feelings, beautiful bodies, precise and evocative words. Spinning outward, a big bang within my frozen world, these became planets, spheres of influence. "Will you choose us?" they asked repeatedly. "Will you choose *us*?"

A man or woman who is near death, unconscious, may hear human voices like aural shadows, and may—if the possibility of choice still remains in the dying body—decide to accept a new, human life or abandon all that is temporal. Hearing those voices, I find I cannot abandon the world. More than that: I want the world, want its physical hardness and qualities of light and color and sound, the depths of its touch and soul. In the words of poets and teachers I see my own path back into that world.

I stay awake all night, reading the poems of Berry and Fields and N. Scott Momaday. When dawn breaks I feel refreshed, as if I had finally found the long sleep I had craved for months. I fix a bowl of cereal, then head for the dean's office, where I talk my way out of Harvard and arrange to have my tuition returned. I run over to Boston on adrenaline to buy a plane ticket to California. Two days later I walk, as Fields said, "from my dark to a stranger world."

HOW STRANGE IT SEEMED, THEN, TO BE ALIVE. LIFE WAS stranger than the death I had been living; it struck me with an electric force. Ordinary details—a single horse at the top of a ridge near Alpine Road in the California coastal range, the way asphalt crumbled toward a creek bed, the scent of salt air near the intersection of Portola Road and Highway

1—seized me bodily at times, flooding me with the joy of perception. There was so much I had not seen. I bought a used pair of hiking boots in Palo Alto, then lit out for the Point Reyes National Seashore, a sixty-six-thousand-acre pre- serve of mountains and beaches just north of San Francisco. I went back over my old high school routes across the coastal range to the Pacific—but slowly, slowly. I stopped every- where. Where there were trails, I hiked them.

Sometimes, on these long walks, I thought of nothing for hours. At least that is how it seemed. In fact, thoughts passed across my mind, but I was somehow able to let them go. The fear and shame of my own mortality did not obsess me, and in the crisp blue sky of the coastal range I felt myself becoming the air I breathed. I succumbed willingly to all such illusions; they were neither contrived nor sentimental. I lived them; I made contact with the world through them.

At other times, on these walks, I wrapped myself in thought. I was awed at my return from the dead, and humble before whatever constellations of power had conspired with my own choice to liberate me from spiritual despair. I had found a flood of life coming to me from poems and essays. I could not consider them merely in terms of literary structures and historical models; I had to think of them as triggers for a new kind of faith.

As long as words had been mere concepts for me, abstrac- tions, I could not say what I knew; I could not, finally, say whether I knew anything. I was lost in a world of language, where anything was possible. On the Bear Valley trail at Point Reyes, however, where the laurel arched over me with a fragrance not unlike knowledge, I felt as if words too were different: more spare, more limited, more exacting and exact. Nature was not a collection of abstractions, not a temple of Beauty, Grace, Power, Truth. Nature was simply nature. It had its own presence, schedule, instincts. It was not ultimately accessible to the rational mind, yet it was not discontinuous with human life, as some thinkers believed. In its structures, its collapses and renewals, human beings could sense their own fates. I knew, as I walked, that I was where I wanted to be, and that what I said was what I wanted to say. Although the evening sky burned with a luminous fire, there was no inferno at Point Reyes.

Yet the mind is not a linear creature, but cyclic, given to sudden leaps, false starts, and regressions. In October of 1977, I found myself slipping toward despair again. I had my health back for the first time in nearly half a year; my long hikes and my reading of various poets and philosophers appeared to heal me of the worst excesses of my religion. My appetites returned. I began to eat again, and as I recovered I recalled the luxuries of human love. At that point a dark cloud rose again on the horizon. I heard the old voices accusing me of loving what was unreal. Would I never escape these spiritual accusers?

I slump in a chair in Kenneth Fields's old office in Building 30, one of the few unrenovated buildings in the inner quad at Stanford. The two-story ceiling keeps the hot air above us; in the cool afternoon light we read together.

We have been reading Emily Dickinson. We have talked about the erotic imagery in the poem "I started Early—Took my Dog," and about the "power to die" at the end of "My Life had stood—a Loaded Gun." Struggling to distance myself from the subjects under discussion, attempting to recover my literary judgment, I give my mood away. Ken shifts to a different poem:

> There's a certain Slant of light,
> Winter Afternoons—
> That oppresses, like the Heft
> Of Cathedral Tunes—
>
> Heavenly Hurt, it gives us—
> We can find no scar,
> But internal difference,
> Where the Meanings, are—

None may teach it—Any—
'Tis the Seal Despair—
An imperial affliction
Sent us of the Air—

When it comes, the Landscape listens—
Shadows—hold their breath—
When it goes, 'tis like the Distance
On the look of Death—

Ken leans back in his old wooden chair, watching me. "What do you think?" he asks.

I begin to struggle with the language of extension—the language of human beings who seem to reconstruct the world according to their own moods or intuitions, then attribute that world to outside forces, to "slants of light." Ken interrupts.

"Not about that," he says. "I mean about the despair. What do you think about the despair?"

I sit, not quite thinking, my mouth slightly open. I want to say that despair infects the poem, infects the whole world when it descends—infects my world right now as I struggle to sound like a student worthy of respect. But I can't. Ken breaks the silence.

"What do you think Judas's greatest sin was?" he asks.

"What?"

"Judas's greatest sin," he demands. "What was it?"

"Well, of course it was his betrayal of Christ," I say.

"No, no," he replies, speaking softly, leaning forward. "That is one view. But I do not think it is the right view. Judas's greatest sin was not his betrayal of Jesus, which in any case had been foretold. His sin was to give in to despair. He killed himself because he did not believe that God had the power to save his soul. He lost faith in God's love."

The slant of light in the office grows longer, more soothing. Ken leans back in his chair, creaking it to fill the silence. I keep still.

"Dickinson knew what a great danger despair was," he says. "She could see it, feel it, taste it. But she did not give in to it. That's one of the reasons she's a great poet." He waits a moment. "Do you see what I'm saying?"

"I think so," I say. The flames of the inferno recede from around my feet. We say good-bye for the day, and I go home to write my poems.

AT FIRST I WROTE ABOUT GHOSTS, THOUGH NOT MY OWN. Although the tomb which divided me from my past had already begun to crumble, I could not address my own ghost: he was still too close to me, and I had to push him away. Defanged, made separate from me by the enforced winnowing of despair, he receded into the reliquary of darkness, and other spirits emerged. I did not seem to have known them before, although their language sounded familiar. It was the language of possibility, of comfort, divorced from any religious pretense.

Yet, however derived from the spirit, comforting words made the body their home. I felt this, of course, before I was able to put it into words. One day in the depths of my summer abroad I had gone to the Church of Saint Michael and All Angels in Hughendon, England, to pay my respects to the ghost of Benjamin Disraeli. Neither well nor, at that moment, in a state of despair, I was conscious largely of my life of opposition: I seemed to have opposed my parents, my church, and even myself, without necessarily intending to. I was intrigued with the art of opposition as Disraeli practiced it. After touring the remnants of his life in Hughendon Manor, I walked down to St. Michael's.

The church was empty. As I made my way toward the elaborate marble pulpit in the chancel, feeling entirely like an imposter, I awaited the usual impulse to flee. It did not come. Passing my hand over each of the hard oak benches, I found the contact soothing and basic. The light from the deepset neo-Gothic windows had a muted ordinariness that steadied me. It almost seemed a kind of test, though there was no proctor and no right answer.

Climbing the pulpit, I found the Bible opened to Isaiah 40: "Comfort ye, comfort ye my people, saith your God." I read the words to myself. Then I read them aloud in the small echoing church. There was no inrushing of spirit, no murmur like a flock of doves rising to the top of the chancel. I was alone with the wooden benches and the muted light, where the words of comfort traveled from my mouth to the tiniest leading of the nave windows. And yet I felt that I had been visited, in a way completely apart from the legacy of Christian visitations, by a ghostly presence, in the church but not of it, of the sort that might have left a page open to a particular blessing of comfort and guaranteed that no orthodox Christian would intrude upon the moment. If only I could have held that moment.

In a way I did. It stayed in mind, through the fits of despair that summer in England and that fall in Massachusetts, so that later in California I began to look back through my life for other traces of such a presence.

In an old file folder I found a poem I had written three years before. It was a poem of visitation, but also a poem of bodies. Two lovers, trapped in the isolation of their bodies, turn from each other; the man sees, then, that the woman derives comfort from a source he cannot rival.

I stared at the early version. Although its mannered diction wounded the poem, there was something true in it. I wondered, was it an attack on bodies? I read it at first as a poem by a young Christian Scientist, subtly arguing for the primacy of spirit over flesh. But then I saw something else happening in the poem: the spirit cherishes the woman's body. What the man witnesses is not simply his own physical limit, but the presence of the spirit in the flesh. They are not opposed.

I found to my surprise that I was not simply writing about ghosts, but also about bodies. The revisions necessary to clar-

ify this shift in "The Companion" came clearly to me as I
moved through the poem word by word, hearing the next
word in my mind just before I needed it. In a half-hour the
new poem was done.

> Before I turned to you
> It had arrived, companion of the moonlight
> Resting on your troubled face.
>
> Asleep, you could not discern
> The way that it slipped in,
> Without sound, between the window
>
> And the window-frame;
> A mere sense
> Of solitary movement against
>
> The rising storm,
> As sheep on a coastal hill
> Turn one by one from the gale.
>
> More gentle than my touch
> It washed over you, made you stir,
> Brought you in from the wind.

Holding the revision away from me a little, as if to master
a perspective, I saw that—as in the original version—I had
made the protagonist a ghost. The ghost was a "sense," an
opposing presence. In the earlier version of the poem, I could
not seem to decide whether I was using the bodies as props
for a spiritual experience or writing about actual people; the
revision made this clearer. The human beings, and their bodily
experience, became essential. They were not less real than the
comforting spirit. It was the comforting spirit, in fact, which
insisted on their bodily reality.

This comforting spirit, without church or doctrine, appeared as a source of power in several other poems I revised
or wrote in the fall of 1977. I composed these with the passionate intensity of a man insisting that his life meant x and

not *y*: the poems surrounded me like a fortress, keeping the miseries of my dying religion at bay. But the poems were not only a source of comfort; they were a bridge to other people in the Stanford writing workshop who, in reading them, read some truth in me that I had only begun to see. I at first presented my work tentatively, not knowing what kind of person had written it and not yet sure of what it meant to be alive again. The other writers in the workshop saw the ghosts, the sources of mystery and comfort, and taught me what my words were saying. And they responded with poems as well. One of these writers, Michael Ramsey-Perez, seemed particularly sympathetic. His poems also recorded a pilgrimage from the tomb, although his sense of abandonment had a Catholic rather than a Christian Science origin. We were both learning the hard craft of metamorphosis.

I continued my metamorphosis on many evenings with Michael in his studio apartment above a garage in Menlo Park. One of eight children, son of an Army sergeant, Michael knew the taste of betrayal. He told me one day of the woman who had denied him an apartment in a neighboring town because she didn't want all his brothers and sisters moving in with him. "Mexicans do that, you know," she said, as if offering a rational explanation. Betrayed by prejudice, Michael nevertheless excelled in school. In a cruel and frightened society, excellence may be the best single weapon against prejudice. Michael came to Stanford armed with the wide reading and acumen which would bring the rewards of excellence.

But graduate school wore heavily on him; the literature he had loved so much began to feel lifeless under the weight of critical theories and minutiae. He had begun to write poetry only a year or so before I met him, yet within that time he had acquired a lucid, insistent style that made his readers take notice. The only limit on his career, we knew, was the usual one: he would need more luck than he had yet been granted.

Lack of luck was not much on our minds on those evenings in his apartment. The bees buzzed loudly in the Cecil

Bruner rose bush outside his windows; the northern breeze brought the scent of apricot trees in the yard behind him. It was a place of peace and beauty. Neither of us had much money, and most of that went for books, so the other necessities became spaghetti, spaghetti sauce, and beer for Michael. Though I would not take my first drink for almost two more years, I enjoyed watching Michael drink, and liked the imaginative possibilities of a contact high. Michael would boil a vat of spaghetti, crack open a can of Safeway's cheapest spaghetti sauce, and warm up to dinner with a beer. Sitting at his rickety table, I would talk myself into smelling the fragrances of delicious food. Michael's cocker spaniel Stranger, the only dog I'd ever met who peed from sheer ecstasy, would pace back and forth in mounting delight until we let him out in the back yard.

After dinner we'd work through his record collection of Jean Ritchie and Joan Baez, then move on to poems—Donne and Herbert, Louise Bogan, Yeats, Wallace Stevens, Gary Soto. We would read our own poems to each other and discuss them; we would read the poems of our friends in the workshop. In the new darkness, words seemed to acquire a weight or density of their own, drawing the night down close around us. We held an unmysterious seance with the real. Later, depending on how much beer Michael had had and how much I had pretended to have, we would widen our reading: we once came close to choking on our laughter while reciting the first page of *Zen Mind, Beginner's Mind* with the wrong attitude (though, thinking of the author, Shunryu Suzuki, I now wonder if he might not have been pleased). At the end of the evening, before Michael collapsed into bed and I staggered out to my 1964 VW for the drive home, we sang a few of the songs we'd heard earlier. We sang with great passion. Michael especially took pride in his rich, campfire voice, and labored over it as if he were polishing a stone.

Having not had a close male friend since high school, I had forgotten the pleasure of simply hanging around. I had also forgotten how creative hanging around could be—how easily it could breed ideas or poems. Michael, who shared more of my suffering and my ambition than anyone else I knew, helped keep my old ghosts of despair at bay; yet he knew the power of the angels, as he called them, and understood before I did that my pale and protestant "sense" in "The Companion" was the beginning of a body of spirit in my life. In his own life, he sought the angels of a wider integration—an immanence of spirit that did not deny or judge the body.

One evening, slowly making our way toward our own poems, we spent some time reading Wallace Stevens. After "Sunday Morning" and "The Snow Man," we moved to the later poems; my favorites were "The World as Meditation" and "Large Red Man Reading."

"Let's do 'Large Red Man,' " Michael said, and so we did. In the cool of the evening, as Michael read, each line flared into meaning.

There were ghosts that returned to earth to hear his phrases,
As he sat there reading, aloud, the great blue tabulae.
They were those from the wilderness of stars that had expected more.

A realm of disappointed ghosts, I thought to myself. Are these my ghosts, or different ones? Are they the ghosts of possibility?

There were those that returned to hear him read from the poem of
    life,
Of the pans above the stove, the pots on the table, the tulips among
    them.
They were those that would have wept to step barefoot into reality,

The poem of life—was that not what Michael and I were reading, in words and in our actions? The red man was the living man, and the ghosts coveted his life, the blood-richness of his being: his life was the one life, the embodied spirit.

That would have wept and been happy, have shivered in the frost
And cried out to feel it again, have run fingers over leaves
And against the most coiled thorn, have seized on what was ugly

Seized on what was ugly—no, I said to myself, that cannot
be, thinking of the times I had impaled my fingers on roses,
remembering that prick of life even now.

And laughed, as he sat there reading, from out of the purple tabulae,
The outlines of being and its expressings, the syllables of its law:
Poesis, poesis, the literal characters, the vatic lines,

Which in those ears and in those thin, those spended hearts,
Took on color, took on shape and the size of things as they are
And spoke the feeling for them, which is what they had lacked.

" 'The purple tabulae,' " Michael said, staring at the rose
outside the window.

"The red man plus the blue tabulae," I said. "Red plus blue
equals purple. Reading the world changes you, gives you life."

"Or more than life," Michael said. "Purple is a royal color.
The color of royalty. Majesty."

We went on to other poems, and songs, as the evening
evolved. They were not as memorable, however, as the idea
of majesty, a simple enough concept that seemed at first to
have nothing to do with Michael's run-down studio or our
presence in it. I still did not understand how commonplace
life could be majestic. I did not consciously accept the possibility that any ordinary gesture or moment could harbor the
holy ghost, the immanent spirit I had begun to identify in
my poems. Yet there was majesty around us as we read that
night. It was poor enough and humble enough that I simply
overlooked it. But it did not overlook me.

IT HAS BEEN TWELVE YEARS SINCE MICHAEL AND I TALKED OF majesty and ghosts in his tiny studio. The ghosts, or what I have called ghosts, in my own life have begun to resolve themselves into orbits. They have a gravitational force that draws me back toward them, depending on the intensity of my own emotional state. Even before she died, for example, my mother had become a kind of ghost: she cast her lot with a religion that I could no longer tolerate, that I remembered mostly as a source of fear in our household. We were afraid of everything—afraid of sickness, afraid of deviating from God's word, afraid of mortal mind, afraid of the body, afraid of sex, afraid of people, of difference, of strangers, even of love. In truth, no one could blame all of these fears on Christian Science, or any religion. Indeed, I initially cast my religion in terms of my family, rather than the other way around. I see now, however, how much influence our religion had on these fears. Christian Science taught the complete power of divine Love, insisting on the power of Love to heal every mental and physical illness. When no healings came, the language of the religion broke down.

If, as we were taught, the "science" of Christian Science was always perfect, any failing must have a human origin: the individual patient or practitioner must have failed. But how could divine Love permit such failure? It could not, of course; thus the patient or practitioner had somehow shown a particular susceptibility to mortal mind, the illusory power which suggests that the physical world is real. Yet, because the routes to healing in Christian Science are understood to be infinitely diverse, no practitioner is ever held responsible for a failed healing, and there is no method by which to critique the practitioner's prayer; one simply declares the unreality of the failed healing and seeks the stronger faith that heralds future success.

For us, however, a shadow question lay behind this quest. When would mortal mind strike? Would it strike when my mother had a stroke, in the fall of 1977; or when I tore the skin near my knee down to the bone in a bicycle accident in 1969? It seemed that mortal mind had a propensity for striking whenever divine Love was needed most. The world was a frightening place: one had the words of divine Love, but one could never be sure of the outcome. And Christian Science had no words for failed outcomes. There was no comfort, no forgiveness. Perhaps that is why, in the last weeks of her life in 1976, as she was dying of cancer, my grandmother Naner abandoned her Christian Science faith and returned to her Southern Baptist roots. My sister, who was with her at the time, reported the event with some wonder.

"She told me Christian Science offers no comfort for the dying," Cin said. "Imagine that. A former practitioner saying that."

When, like Naner, I pulled away, I pulled away from the reality my mother embraced. There was little meeting ground between us, only silence. This silence filled the air of the high entryway when I came to the Christian Science care home in San Francisco for my weekly or semiweekly visits to my mother. It infected the corridors of the second floor, where patients with "special needs" were removed from the other Christian Scientists who came to the home for a few days of rest and spiritual study.

My father and Lesley and I were the three members of the family to visit my mother regularly. My sister, who lived in Maine, came twice; my brother, who lived in Los Altos, came once and vowed never to return. ("That place is like a living death," he said to me in a rare moment of candor.) The Christian Science practitioner who prayed for my mother came infrequently, preferring to offer her prayers by telephone. When she did come, she arrived like a small whirlwind, asking my mother why she was not up and around, why she had not eaten, why she did not get dressed. My mother, who reported this to me, took these exhortations to mean that she had failed once again. In the last six weeks of her life, when she had difficulty speaking or lifting the telephone receiver, my mother simply refused to take the practitioner's calls.

My father had brought my mother a cassette player for her favorite music. When she could no longer push the buttons, she would sometimes gesture for me to help her. She would often do this during the evening prayer service, which was piped in from the chapel through a speaker at her bedside. The old, dying Christian Scientists, raising their ruined voices in hymns they had sung since childhood, were almost too gruesome to bear. My mother, who knew all of Mary Baker Eddy's hymns and their musical arrangements by heart, came to prefer secular songs. Yet even these songs could horrify. One evening, following her hand signals, I pushed the button on the cassette recorder and heard "You Needed Me," a song of good-bye in which the singer thanks the departing lover for his devotion. It was, I suddenly realized, my father's good-bye to my mother. His religion forbad him to admit the end; he had to say good-bye obliquely, in song. I began to cry. My mother looked at me, but could not speak.

A few days later I brought her a poster of Picasso's *Child Holding a Dove,* a painting I knew she loved. She had modeled a portrait of my sister on this painting. She seemed almost to smile; it was the one connection she and I had left, the mystery of beauty in an imperfect world. Then I brought a book of spiritual direction from a Catholic priest, which I had found the previous spring at Canterbury Cathedral. The book had comforted me recently; I wanted to offer it to her. I could no longer use the language of Christian Science, which had failed so utterly and left her in such pain, but I wanted to offer some vision of comfort. I began to read. With excruciating slowness, she turned away from me. She did not look or acknowledge my departure when I left. We had become ghosts to each other. Thought and language had divided us. I was no longer her dutiful son, and she was no longer the mother whose passion and artistry promised rewards that she would not live to acquire.

As much as I seemed to irritate her, she pointed to the Picasso poster when I came the next time, indicating that she wanted it near her bed as long as she was there. And then, after my efforts to console her with my own religious words and those of others had failed, I would simply sit with her in the foul-smelling room of the care home, where outside the window a sweet fog swept through the stands of eucalyptus. One clear evening, in an act of almost scorching clarity, she stopped running her crippled hand through her hair and pointed insistently to the full moon. I understood, but was too well-trained to say good-bye—and too embarrassed to cry again.

"Don't worry," I said, "I'll be back in a few days." I never saw her again.

I tried to think of that evening as the end of the lie for her, as the fulfillment of what her authentic life had amounted to, where her body had brought her, and where the spirit inter-woven in that body would lead her. Yet this was not the end of the lie; there was one final episode to make burden heavier. My father, torn between his instincts and his desire to be faithful to his religion, had scheduled a business trip to New York on October 29, 1980. As he explained to me later, in tears, he asked the Christian Science nurses at the care home whether he ought to postpone or cancel his trip. No one was indiscreet enough to mention death; nevertheless, my father understood that they were all talking about the same thing. The nurses, however, reminded him that his wife was in God's care, and that he should live his life in the full expec-tation of her spiritual health. He interpreted this to mean that he should travel. He arrived in New York on the 29th, in the early evening. Around five-thirty the following morning, New York time, he called me. My mother had died about an hour and a half before, as near as anyone knew, he told me wearily. He was flying back as soon as possible.

Lesley and I lay in bed together, talking quietly. I seemed

for the time being to have no tears left to cry for my mother; I wept for my father. Despite their difficulties and differences, my father had wanted most of all to be with my mother at her dying, to demonstrate his final faithfulness. The well-intended rhetoric of Christian Science had deprived him even of this last consolation. The perfection of the religion had produced, not more perfection, but misery.

Since death is unreal in the religion, Christian Science makes no provision for funeral services and offers no specific comfort for the relatives of the dead. Shortly after my mother died, the branch church that she and my father had attended for eleven years sent my father a letter for comfort. In this letter they exhorted him to remember that the spiritual ideal of my mother remained perfect and eternal. It was a sign of his desperate need for human consolation and attention that he tacked the letter up on the refrigerator and pointed it out to me every time we walked through the kitchen. How he might have liked a gathering of the community for his sake, a service in his wife's memory! Instead he received a letter. The letter was, in a sense, addressed to me as well, because its "truths" against mourning the dead affected me directly: I was not supposed to mourn, because my mother had simply "passed on"; I could take comfort in the unblemished spiritual fact of her continued existence; there was no cause for grief, which was an effect of mortal mind.

I tried to talk myself out of grieving. I thought I had left the religion behind, yet in the face of my mother's death I ran back to its familiar words: I did not grieve. A year later, I began to have terrible nightmares. I developed an obsessive fear of newly turned earth. I could not plant seeds in the garden for fear I would turn up a body. It seemed that I walked over incarnate ghosts, only weakly buried in weak earth; the least effort on my part would bring them to the surface. Eventually the fear grew even more precise, more horrible. I was afraid that I had killed someone, perhaps many people, without knowing it. I was afraid that I was a murderer. Although I knew rationally that I had never done such things, the ghosts that haunted my mind made reason for a time irrelevant. For a few months I lived in terror of what I could not possibly have done.

In retrospect it seems hard to believe that I was more or less able to function. I had recently become a graduate student in English at the University of California, Berkeley, and during this crisis I managed to produce competent work. Because ordinary life was a nightmare, however, I finally took myself to the psychological counseling services at the university health center.

When I first talked to a therapist on the staff at the health center, I was struck by the number of questions she asked about my mother. How had she died? Was there a funeral? What are the basic beliefs of Christian Science? How would I describe my relationship with my mother? I wanted to talk about my nightmares, my fear of unearthing dead bodies or of murdering people; we did talk of this, but largely in passing. I left that first session confused—not at all sure I had done the right thing in seeking such help.

A few days later I had a session with a consulting psychiatrist—a child psychiatrist. Although I thought this was a little odd, I was grateful for the attention, since both my therapist and the psychiatrist were actually asking me questions about my life instead of telling me the "truths" I had heard for years from practitioners. At the end of the hour, moderately distraught, I asked the psychiatrist for her impression of me.

"You haven't hurt anyone," she said. "But I think there's a major issue of anger to be dealt with here."

I must have looked confused. I wasn't angry at anyone—just terrified of myself.

"You know," she continued, "one of the things we do with children who have trouble with anger is to bring them into a room with their parents. They can yell and scream at their parents, they can say 'I want to kill you!,' they can hit their parents with pillows. After all that, they see that they haven't hurt their parents physically. Their anger hasn't killed their parents. Their anger is something about them, and about their relationship with their parents. It's not some magical weapon. It has no magical powers."

"You're saying that I'm angry at my mother?" I asked. "For what? For dying? For making me a Christian Scientist? For not healing me when I was sick? You're saying I'm angry at God?"

"I think you have a lifetime of anger," she said, "and it will take time to sort it all out. I know how painful your fears are, but it's good that you've come here. It means you're ready to work on what you've been through."

I was now frightened of what I had set in motion. What would I discover about myself? About my parents? My religion? Perhaps I was at heart an awful person, a despicable character. Further sessions of therapy led me into deep trepidation. I was, after all, in uncharted waters; if medicine was considered incompatible with Christian Science, mental health services were unspeakable. They used mortal mind to treat the disease of mortal mind, instead of trying to eradicate that "illusory" mind. Nevertheless, I continued the sessions, and as I progressed I found myself overcome with an intense mourning for my mother. I left each session in tears; I cried uncontrollably for a half-hour each evening. This went on for about a week. After that, for reasons which seemed inexplicable to me, the ghosts began to recede. My fears of dead bodies and murder eased; I spent more time discussing my family, my religion, and my own relationship with them. Thus the ghosts of my past became way stations on my own journey toward a discrete identity. As they receded, I became someone new. This newness seemed to be a matter of drawing closer to the child I had been at heart—the creator of cities, the motorcyclist, the poet who eyed the world critically and knew by instinct what was true and what was false.

I also became, as the child psychiatrist had predicted, angrier than I had ever been before. In a therapist's quiet office in a beautiful part of Oakland, a couple of miles south of the university campus, I found myself rising repeatedly toward rage. I witnessed, as if for the first time, the panorama of my life: the shame I felt as a child because I was not like the other children who went to doctors and got well, the fear that stalked my spiritualized and abstracted household, the denial of the body, the love in word but too rarely in deed. There was no one to punish: there were only ghosts. Yet they were my ghosts now. I had begun to take charge of them. For many years they had ruled me. They had made me feel guilty for not being "perfect"; they had made me doubt my human reality. They might, from time to time, draw me back to those dangerous perigees in moments of crisis, but they could never again rule me. I had—perhaps for the first time in my life—a sovereign, conscious mind, mortal though it might be. And I would not easily relinquish that gift.

In my poems, I began to carve out a language of body and spirit that drew me back to the world, away from the religion that had caused me so much unacknowledged grief. Until I could acknowledge that grief, however—until I could rid myself of the guilt of having failed in my faith—even the poems could not save me. Even art—in which I had placed so much hope, as my mother had, seeking an alternative reality to the "reality" of her faith—could not heal me of a rage I could not bring myself to admit. The ghosts behind my rage—the ghosts of my childhood, my religion, my fear—moved silently in their orbits, disinterested, aware that poems could touch them but not shake their hold. And yet the impulse that led me to poetry—the impulse to speak truly about the body and its mind—led me as well to a kind of healing I had never known before.

What I lacked as a young poet was a methodology. I thought I could shift my allegiance from my religion to poetry without losing either one; I would float between them, drawing on the best of each. I could not admit to myself that an allegiance to poetry meant a questioning of orthodoxy. Authentic poetry is true only to its own clearest insights: it advances no ideology, serves no religion or political vision or cause. My inability to come to terms with Christian Science marred my insights, and kept me in chains even as I began to experiment with the language of ghosts and bodies. I did not have the strength to invent a method of self-analysis, nor could I face my rising perceptions of my past reality. I could not admit the rage. Thus I continued to write in a voice at times tame and formal, at other times unshaped, confused, and ominous. Only in the last few years have I begun to make my peace with that rage, and hear the faint traces of a unified, whole voice.

And I have begun to learn how to keep the ghosts of my past at bay. I take comfort in the notion of a divine absence, and in the love of specific people. Perhaps I crave a divine absence and a human presence because that is exactly the opposite of what I received as a child: I now prefer human love because for so many years I did not feel that I had it. It still seems too easy to talk about "ghosts," about "holy presences," as if such words clearly meant only one thing. Whatever that holy presence is, it is infinitely various—and ultimately, I think, not ghostly. It is not something pale in the distance, nor is it a slight quiver in the heart, or a quaver in the air. It is keen and definite, like a kiss or an orgasm. I look back with some tenderness on my poems of ten or twelve years ago, but they do not seem strong enough, hard enough, to me. They do not have the reality that Warren Wilde tried to give me even earlier, when I could not possibly have understood him and yet—at some hard, bedrock level of the soul—did.

Looking up from my keyboard, I see that it is now early afternoon; the morning has passed unnoticed as I traveled the old routes of my life. It feels suddenly as if I have arrived, not at a destination, but at a significant way station—an unmarked oasis not on my original map. It is the kind of place where one changes from a car to a Land Rover, and checks over one's provisions: the terrain shifts from grasslands to desert up ahead. One says good-bye to old acquaintances, and hopes for a good night's rest. The next phase of the journey will be strenuous, though in some odd way perhaps not as strenuous as the trip here.

7

SOURCES

Books, like people, have histories of their own. They are complete only in relation to their past. This book began two years ago, in the fall of 1988, when I moved from California to Boston and suddenly felt that I had left my real life, whatever that was, behind. I wrote as a form of morning meditation, five pages a day, before the start of my other day of fatherhood and teaching. At first the book seemed simply a way of recovering my own history in the face of psychic and geographic disruption. I had not foreseen the other kinds of disruption that might evolve from this. After about a month of writing, the nightmares began, interrupting my sleep with images more frightening than I had seen in years.

Among the worst of these was a recurrent dream of assault, in which I, as a young boy, tried to elude a large dark man in black clothing. Though I ran as fast as I could, panting and disoriented, he moved with the deliberateness of one whose aim was clear. In each of these dreams I ran into a dark shed, hoping to hide; in each dream he entered the shed, filling the doorway with his darkness, then slowly moving toward me. In successive dreams he drew closer, touching me, tearing at my clothes as I tried to scream but made no sound. I would awaken in a fierce sweat with a sense of darkness which the day only gradually assuaged. I had had these dreams, less vivid and less often, as a child and as a young man; their current intensity made the book an impossible project. I could not continue to write. And so, with about a hundred pages drafted, I threw the book in a file drawer and tried to forget it.

But by then the book was bound up in my life, and the kind of meditation it had set in motion stayed with me. A year and a half later I opened the file drawer again, and found a manuscript filled with imperfections—griefs, rages, wounds, bodily love and love of the soul, and cries for God which seemed only randomly heard. To someone trained, as I was, to see the perfect spirituality of creation, these imperfections were deeply threatening. Yet as I grew accustomed to thinking about what I finally chose to think about—my authentic responses to pain and falsehood, to illness, and to love—I began to find a kind of comfort in imperfection. The imperfect does not, at least, point toward a higher or truer reality. It is not a chorus of gratitude to God.

Perhaps it *is* God. In its record of suffering, in its tawdry acceptance of the fully human, in its forgiveness, in its promise and granting of solace, this imperfection creates the panorama in which Jesus once appeared because he knew that the human world was also divine, a home and a point of departure. The man who angrily threw the money changers from the temple, who listened to the voices of temptation, who despaired of his God at the last, was an imperfect man who knew the divine spirit rested precisely within his imperfection, his humanity. In the end he had to be content, not with love, but with truth—the truth of his own condition. And this saved him: ironically, this brought him back to love.

EVEN EARLY IN MY LIFE, I UNDERSTOOD THAT MY PARENTS WERE imperfect, and that the Father-Mother God was not like them—or any other human parents—was not like anything knowable at all. And yet this did not change my faith in perfection. God was the perfect father and mother. He and She were a series of abstractions on the one hand, and on the other a kind of comforting sound, the nuzzling sound a baby makes, for example, without meaning and yet somehow a blessing. I taught myself to take comfort in this image of flawlessness. When I first saw that my parents gained strength in division, in separateness, I wondered whether there was some fundamental flaw in their relationship to God, but my doubt simply coexisted with the Christian Science teaching that nothing interrupts the all-harmonious relationship between humankind and God. Years later, after I had endured numerous failed healings and other miseries, and after I had discovered the deep consolations of the body, I still held on to this faith in perfection. I practiced a form of mental apartheid: my empirical reality of love and loss and struggle abutted the Christian Science reality of perfect spirit, but the two never mingled. Over time, the gulf between them grew habitual; eventually it appeared unbridgeable. Even in times of crisis my doubts penetrated only so far against my faith.

When I was a sophomore in college, I began to act on my desire to become a Christian Science practitioner. I pursued this goal in part from a wish to heal others, in part from a profound need to protect myself. If I became a practitioner, some distant part of me reasoned, I would gain access to the holy truth which my messy human life kept obscuring. I would no longer suffer the physical and psychological miseries of my past. I would be the physician who could heal himself.

In Christian Science, a small number of experienced practitioners become teachers of the religion. These teachers

conduct intensive, two-week-long training sessions each year
for Christian Scientists who wish to practice spiritual healing.
To be admitted to one of these sessions, known as class instruction (or simply "class" among Christian Scientists), is
considered a sign of spiritual maturity. Articles on the subject
regularly appear in the *Christian Science Journal,* encouraging
readers to pray earnestly for the insight which will lead them
to the right teacher at the right time.

In the fall of 1976 I felt that I had examined my relationship
with God rather carefully: I accepted the reality of my perfect
spiritual identity, unharmed by the competing claims of mortal mind, and felt that God's divine harmony might well work
through me to heal others of the misconceptions of human
existence. The Christian Science teacher I felt compelled to
query was a forthright and gentle man who practiced at that
time in San Francisco. He had previously been an editor of
the *Christian Science Sentinel* and the *Christian Science Journal,*
and I had studied his writings on Christian Science for several
years. His understanding of the religion seemed unusually
clear to me, and devoid of the sentimental rhetoric that seemed
to infect so much of the other writing in those publications.
Admiring his work and learning from it, I thought I might
present myself to him as a candidate for class instruction.
After I wrote to inquire about the possibilities, describing
what I took to be my qualifications—my regular Sunday
school and church attendance, my devoted study of the Bible
and the writings of Mary Baker Eddy, and my interest in
becoming a practitioner—he invited me to San Francisco for
an interview.

From the articles I had read in the *Journal* I believed that
the interview itself would be a source of blessing, and as I
drove toward San Francisco I found myself constantly reading
the world around me for signs of spiritual truth. It was a
typically beautiful fall day. The tawny hills along Highway
280 seemed to glow with a light inferior only to the light of
the sun itself, and as I approached Daly City the ocean of

gray fog above the coastal range spilled over the land in vast, slow undulations. One could read spiritual reality—Beauty, Grace, even Truth—in such a landscape.

At Daly City I parked the car and switched to the local rapid transit system, BART. I had brought with me a copy of the current *Christian Science Herald,* the foreign-language compendium of the other religious periodicals. Although the *Herald* is published in many languages, I was studying French in college, and so attempted to master Christian Science and French at the same time. As my BART train made its way toward the Embarcadero station in San Francisco, I read through the articles in the *Herald,* checking the facing-page English version now and then for difficult words. Then I came upon a phrase that seemed written for me. After praying intently, the author of this particular article still remained unhealed. In a moment of profound humility, she wrote, she turned to God and simply asked, "Montre-moi ce que j'ai besoin d'apprendre"—"Show me what I need to learn."

I stopped reading the *Herald* and, in preparation for the interview, tried to open my thought to the divine Voice. It seemed better, somehow, to do this in a language other than English: English was too close to me, too bound up in my flawed past, to work well now. "Mon Dieu," I said silently, "Montre-moi ce que j'ai besoin d'apprendre." I repeated this thought from time to time as I walked from the station to the forty-story skyscraper in which the teacher had his office.

The teacher was not as I imagined him to be. Though tall, he was slightly stooped, and his odd manner—now deferential, now utterly direct—made him seem less of a physical presence than he might otherwise have been. He struck me as a man of contradictions, although I tried to subsume this thought immediately in my admiration for his work and his distinguished position in the church.

We spent about an hour talking that day. I described my life, being careful to portray it in as positive a light as possible,

and my interest in Christian Science. We talked about childhood, he spoke warmly of his own upbringing, and we discussed my interest in mountain climbing, an interest he had
once shared but never acted on.

"I'm sure you could still pick it up," I said, only half joking (he must have been in his late fifties or early sixties at the
time). His response surprised me.

"I might have started thirty years ago," he said with a
smile. "But I'm not what I once was." Because he spoke with
an honesty that took me aback, I looked for signs of irony.
He seemed completely sincere.

Although I could not quite fathom what appeared to be his
acknowledgement of the limitations of his body, I decided to
be grateful for his candor. When we turned to the subject of
Christian Science, however, his manner changed. Where before he had looked at me directly, he now looked down, or
over my head, or closed his eyes: his religious words took
him away from me. He spoke with a kind of diffidence, a
keen, flat clarity, almost automatically and yet with enough
intonation to make his sincerity clear. He believed what he
was saying, but it seemed to embarrass him; he was uncomfortable with the language. This was not, I felt, the man I
knew from the articles in the *Journal*. Still, I was honored to
have met him, and when the hour was up he offered me an
application for class instruction. I had passed the first hurdle;
I had impressed him with my sincerity, my desire. I left his
office filled with joy.

Instead of driving straight home after I got back to Daly
City, I decided to take Highway 1 down the coast until I felt
compelled to turn inland. I might go as far as Pescadero, I
thought, or Davenport or Santa Cruz; it did not matter. What
mattered was my ability to listen for the divine Voice, to learn
both actually and metaphorically which way to go.

Beyond the tawdry suburb of Pacifica, the road wound
through eucalyptus and laurel, and then down to Devil's Slide,
where the pavement clung to a notch in a sheer cliff. I drove
onward, past the little airport at Princeton Harbor and the

agricultural town of Half Moon Bay, until I was back in the
deep coastal country I loved, the unmarred hills and fields of
artichokes and broccoli running down to the sea. I found
myself praying all the while, repeating the words from the
Herald in my head as I moved through my cherished landscape
and awaited the presence of God.

After a few more minutes of driving, I pulled to the side
of the road where a dirt turnout brought me near the edge
of a cliff. Walking to what appeared to be the edge, I found
that, in fact, I was not quite there: a small grassy ledge angled
downward until it merged with a narrow path to the beach,
allowing me to sit in relative safety a couple of hundred feet
above the surf as I scanned the sand and the waves. I sat.
What I knew, at that moment, was that some kind of meaning
would come to me to confirm everything that I had just
experienced—my new prayer from the *Herald,* my good fortune with the Christian Science teacher, my seemingly promising future as a practitioner, and more—my ardent hope,
despite all that had happened in my life, that I was myself
spiritual and cherished. Perhaps, I thought, all that had gone
before was a kind of test of faith, like Jesus' temptations in
the wilderness; perhaps now, despite my falterings, I would
be redeemed. I watched and waited.

I saw the unsullied sand, the blue-green waves churning
into surf, the gulls hovering at eye level, the beauty I considered emblematic of perfection. And then I saw the naked
man. Even from a hundred yards away he looked like an
athlete: his wide, bronze shoulders gleamed in the late-morn-
ing sun, and his broad chest and thighs showed the strength
of a weight lifter. He was not out for a walk; he puffed and
pranced on the beach like a race horse, although there was
no one to admire him, and when he ran the sand churned
behind him like a wake. He would stop, and pant, and prance,
and turn around; and in an instant of acceleration the sun
would streak along his clenched fist and arm and down the
hard muscles of his buttocks, thighs, and calves, spinning out
in particles of light behind his feet.

I stared in revulsion. It was inconceivable that such a creature should invade the fertile ground I had made for God.
Perhaps a man alone, in khaki pants and a loose-fitting shirt,
walking pensively at the edge of the sand, or a man and a
woman lost in thought—but not this unabashed physical
specimen. What did this man have to do with me or my
spiritual desires? He was an affront to everything I had prayed
for on this day. "Montre-moi ce que j'ai besoin d'apprendre,"
I murmured, standing up at the cliff's edge. As I prepared to
leave, I reaffirmed in my thought the spirituality of God's
creation.

And yet I could not quite leave. For a few seconds I watched
this man run. Far from admiring the precision of his muscles
or the stillness of his torso as he moved his legs, I rejected
them: they could hold no sway over me, for they were not
real. But they remained interesting in their unreality. The
man reached the far end of the beach, turned, and began to
run back toward me. As he passed below me he looked up,
saw me, stared for a fraction of a second, then looked back
down. In the moment our eyes met I saw in his an utter
indifference: not hatred, not shame, not surprise, but a simple
lack of concern for me and my presence there. I had been
noted; I was irrelevant.

Climbing back into the car, I drove several miles south to
a quiet beach with sand dunes, where a few cars littered the
parking lot and promised a minor, comforting crowd. I
grabbed my lunch of cheese and bread, the *Herald,* and my
windbreaker, and wandered back into the dunes until I found
a protected cove where the beach grass rose high above me.
There I sat and ate, and read the *Herald,* looking for clues to
what had gone wrong. I had asked God to show me what I
needed to learn. He was no practical joker; why, then, had
my moment of kinship with Him been ruined? To dwell on
this event, I realized, would be to give credence to the claims
of mortal mind and physical reality. Putting the solitary runner from my mind, I read and prayed in the noonday sun
until my head ached and I felt dizzy. A wind had sprung up,

and the day no longer seemed as delightful or meaningful as it once had been. It was a long walk down the dunes to the car. I took the shortest way home.

That evening and the next day I filled out the Christian Science teacher's application for class instruction. I mailed it immediately; he replied several weeks later. After prayerful consideration, he said, he had decided that I was not an appropriate candidate for his class. My desire to become a practitioner remained for a time, and once or twice I considered applying to a different teacher, but something about my first experience stopped me. It had been at once too promising, too full of portents, and too disturbing to yield anything but a mild catharsis. Yet, as I drew closer to the time when Christian Science would leave me at the gate of misery, I continued to hope that somehow I would hear the divine Voice, and would have an answer to my increasingly plaintive supplication: "Mon Dieu, montre-moi ce que j'ai besoin d'apprendre."

ALL THIS TIME, AS I TRIED TO LISTEN TO THE DIVINE VOICE I had been trained to hear in Christian Science, another voice, equally divine but rich with its different music, was singing to me. It sang as I sat beside the cliff where a naked man pranced into my picture of spiritual perfection. It sang to me through the body of the man himself, through his muscles and sinews and exuberance, saying to me, "It is alright to be a man; it is alright to be a body; it is alright to be human." And I could not accept this voice, because it went against so much of what I had been taught. "Show me what I need to learn," I entreated God in two different languages, hoping for an answer that would coincide with my religious faith. That answer never came. But *an* answer *did* come, repeatedly and consistently. It sang itself into my early years, when I could not choose to hear it, and into my later years, when I could choose but did not know how. Divine, utterly patient, and loving, it never gave up on me, despite my doctrinal stubbornness and timidity and nervous exhaustion.

It was not until I began to weave this book together that I saw the presence of this voice of imperfection, this voice of the divine body, in my life. At first, when I began to write, I wrote chronologically, passing back through events as they had happened. I expected my life to reveal its secrets in this way. Yet as the book evolved, chronology seemed less and less important: what mattered was not a sequence of events, but one event seen over and over at different moments from different vantage points. That one event was the advent of bodily knowledge, of human comfort, which alone for me carried a weight of spiritual power. Too paradoxical for Christian Science, even heretical, the divinity of the body repeated itself to me over and over, and yet I could not or would not listen.

Unwillingly, as if by accident, I sometimes thought of the man on the beach in the weeks before my mother died. He became a strange, unidentifiable harmony behind the silence that had become Christian Science.

Would it have been less cruel, I asked myself, if my mother had gone to a physician, perhaps chosen chemotherapy, perhaps declined further and finished her days in a ward for the terminally ill? Surely that seems cruel as well. But death often seems cruel, whether it is or not. It is the fundamental and final evidence that we are creatures of transformation, that we are not one perfect and eternal identity but evolving identities, subject to change not only in the relative familiarity of one form—the body—but in forms we cannot know or imagine.

For many people, the only antidote to this wretched parting is the kind of love and knowledge that lies within human experience. To have known and understood my mother's illness, to have been with her and spoken with her in the honest language of parting, to have witnessed some final acknowledgement of husband and wife—these would have made her departure less cruel for me. And, in that world of human imperfection, there might have been alternatives where in Christian Science there were none: her cancer might have been excised through surgery or coerced into remission; she might have entered a hospice which, in her last days, could have imparted strength and peace to her and her family. I could not make these possibilities come true in my mother's life, but at least I could begin to distinguish the blessedness of her imperfection from the cruelty of the perfect spiritual identity she had had preached to her until the end. And yet that distinction could not really take hold until I began to write, and to see the presence of God in a man whose nakedness I took to be an affront to my own spirituality.

ALL OF THE IMPERFECTIONS WHICH SHAPED MY LIFE, OFTEN WITHOUT my knowing it, were important, but perhaps the greatest of these was love. I caught a glimpse of this imperfect love when my mother warmed salt in a sock to ease the pain of my infected ear, and when she finally rushed me off to the doctor when I had bronchitis. The limits of this love always seemed to yield some kind of knowledge—knowledge which was specific and helpful, never abstract. Another glimpse of this imperfect love came from Warren Wilde, and still another from my friends in high school. But Lesley was the essential source.

When I left home for college in 1974, the stresses which had evolved from my religious faith and the general uncertainty of my life made a long-term relationship with Lesley seem impossible. I pretended that I had gone halfway around the world, that my life had begun anew and Lesley had been a part of an older world I hoped to jettison. Perhaps, I told myself as I read Plato and Aristotle in the lonely sunshine of the inner quad at Stanford, I could even recover the spirituality I had lost through my love of the body. After a term of intellectual gamesmanship and loneliness, however, I was ready to seek the solace to which I still could not give a name.

Lesley and I eased back into being a pair; yet my selfishness, and the sense of danger that evolved from it, could not easily be eradicated. By the beginning of the following autumn, when Lesley went off to Swarthmore, the tables were turned: she was the one beginning a new life, and I was the holdover, the drag on her future. I flew out once to visit her, saw her room in Willetts Hall and took her to see my old house in West Chester, about ten miles away. We hung around in the evenings with her new friends, who introduced me to each other as Lesley's "boyfriend from California." It was clear that I had no role in this new drama. At Christmas, on a long walk along McClure's Beach at Point Reyes, we agreed to end what had not, in fact, been a relationship for more than two months. At the time this definite answer seemed less like the end of love and more like a simple relief, a form of precision: at least we could say to each other what we felt.

A year went by; we neither saw each other nor called nor wrote. Running into each other one summer day in 1976 on Los Altos Avenue, we asked a few of the usual questions and gave the usual answers. Lesley had left behind the leather skirts and peasant blouses of high school for tee-shirts and denim overalls. Her long blonde hair fell nearly to her waist. Across our wounded distance I could see her beauty, and beneath that something of the person I had once loved. I was angry, although I could not admit it and did not even know why, and I could not quite get her out of my mind. Later that year, when I became desperately afraid for my soul and fearful of all that I had felt for Lesley and had done with her, I wondered if—after so much time had passed—she might speak to me, or be able to comfort me in some way. But I could not call her; I was too embarrassed of my desperation.

In November of 1977, after I had begun my ascent from the mortal darkness of summer, I saw Lesley again. We bumped into each other on State Street in Los Altos. She had come back for the weekend for her grandparents' fiftieth wedding anniversary, she said. How was I? What had I been doing? No longer desperate, experienced in the ways of ghosts, I spoke casually and happily, as if nothing were at stake. I was writing poems, I said; I was hiking in the hills; I had been on trails and routes we had talked about in high school. High school seemed a long way back, and yet in the crisp autumn light it also became the present, as if all the changes had brought us back to a moment before we had caused each other pain. A wariness came over us in the midst of this intricate luxury.

Across the street an art gallery was showing a limited edition of a book by Samuel Beckett with lithographs by Jasper Johns. Lesley glanced over. "Want to go in?" she asked. We walked into the old building, where the fragrances were new: the scents of handmade paper, of rich inks and pigments, mingled with the mustiness that seemed a comfortable reliquary for our old lives. We walked from display to display, examining the impressions of the letters in the paper, discussing Johns' designs, enjoying Beckett's odd English translations of his French text. It was as if we too were enclosed in these works of art, absorbed as part of the meaning of Beckett and Johns and yet discrete. What brought us together at this moment was outside of us, incidental to our lives and yet intimate; it made us safe. We heard in each other's voice the tone of an old, well-stored love.

But it was a tone merely, competing with the reality of our difference and our years apart. We said good-bye a few days later as friends when Lesley dropped by as I was photographing the covers of two of my favorite books.

"Why are you doing that?" she asked.

"I'm afraid they might get lost," I said.

"What—the books?"

"No—the covers. The designs. Look at the way the dark blue fades into the earth here. The way the orange here contrasts with the line drawing. These are works of art—and they're going to get smashed around and smeared, and people are going to put glasses on them and leave little rings, and pretty soon they won't be beautiful anymore. So I'm going to preserve them this way." I took a few more pictures.

Lesley looked at me with the gaze she reserved for the extremely odd. "The publisher has the originals," she finally said. "Besides, everything dies. Everything fades. Books fade. Even great paintings need to be restored. Why do you worry about this, anyway?"

I suddenly realized I could not explain. It was neurotic: I was afraid of death, of decay. I wanted to surround myself with beautiful things and protect them. I did not trust other people to do it. Ghosts, once again. I stopped.

"Do you think this is stupid?" I asked.

She paused. "Not if it's important to you," she answered. A moment of silence.

"I've got to go," she said. "I'll send you a postcard."

That winter and spring, as we both dated other people and tried to ignore each other, a few strands of communication fell into place: she sent me a postcard, but much later than promised, near the end of her junior year. I had already graduated from Stanford, and had spent my spring writing poems and reading art history in the university library. When she wrote to complain about the hectic end of the semester, the advent of finals and research papers, I copied the title poem from Louise Bogan's *The Blue Estuaries* and sent it to her with a note of consolation. She wrote back with a brief, unexpectedly grateful letter. More postcards passed. In one she announced her plan to drive back to California with a friend, making a clear note of her probable date of arrival. I called her at home that evening.

"I thought I might come over," I said.

"Right away," she said.

What began that evening was our second life together, a life much more attuned to imperfection and anger and disagreement than before. As Lesley sat at one end of her bed in her pale sundress, hugging her knees to her chest, and I sat at the other end, my legs dangling off the edge, we worked our way back through the stories of our loves and departures, our profound dislike for one another and our quests for other lovers. What was it about those other lovers, we wondered aloud, which—as much as we loved them—brought us back to each other? It was a question we could not answer except by tracking the history of our nights on the beach at Pescadero and Point Reyes and our rendezvous after the AFS club dinner in high school years before. We spent a long, luminous evening together.

The wary devotion that emerged between us survived my mother's death and my iceberg grief. It outlasted my withdrawal from the Christian Science Mother Church, my dismal march through graduate school, even my journey across the country at the beginning of a new career. It survived Lesley's turmoil as she struggled to find a workable identity, as she labored in jobs she did not particularly like while trying to decide what kind of life might sustain her, and as she began her own difficult but rewarding graduate studies in art history.

Every adventure in love, even divine love, is a risk: the soul asks for a certainty it knows it cannot have. And yet, in the midst of the inevitable instability of love, one sets events in motion, raising the curtain on an unwritten drama. There was nothing perfect about our drama: it was full of doubts and sadness, of moments when one or both of us threatened to end the show. Yet the knowledge that evolved from this always transformed us in some way, taking us by surprise. How much greater, more present, more precise that was than the language of perfection! The passion which years ago led me to the brink of despair over my own imperfection drew me farther, showing me forms of intelligence that I had not expected to find.

Two years ago I felt buried in a sense of conventionality, as if my life and love and career had brought me simply to a point of stasis. The sense of emptiness which comes with such an intuition of conventionality, however, may also be a sign that what one calls one's life remains largely unexamined: the surface is all one has. To smash through that surface is to endure pain, to raise old angers and hatreds, to confront one's own stupidity and stubbornness and unfulfilled hope. But, I think, it is also to see the new patterns which form in one's own personal history. History is never a single truth, but a study of vantage points. This in itself is an avowal of imperfection: the perfect universe, the spiritual realm in which I lived and moved and had my being as a child, admitted to one truth and by implication one vantage point, although it emphasized the infinite individuality of God's creation.

To watch my own past shift and change as I write it, then, is to see God Himself as a fluid and changing form of love and mind, rather than an absolute or constant. Will this vision of God still comfort me in ten years? Stupid question: it comforts me at this point. It changes as I change. That in itself offers some redemption from the past.

WE HAVE COME BACK, LESLEY AND I, TO THE ISLAND WHERE I began to write this book. Nathaniel (almost four) is with us, along with his new sister Georgia, barely three weeks old. For the first time Nathaniel has found the forests around my sister's house a fertile ground for the imagination: he hunts cartoon characters and bears, protecting the deer and smaller animals from predators. In the late afternoon, when the sun barely slips through the tall pines, the forest is a spooky place. Nathaniel and I search for bad witches and goblins together, and when we find them we chase them down to the ocean with sticks until they disperse in the clear air or drown in the sea. A very satisfying day's work.

Being a father makes the legacy of my childhood—the emphasis on spiritual perfection—seem even more peculiar.

I remember reading articles in Christian Science religious periodicals about how parents prayed to understand their children as reflections of the perfect God in order to heal them of colds, flus, or ear infections. To do such a thing to Nathaniel would be, to my mind, a form of abuse.

For Nathaniel is wonderfully imperfect; his imperfection is part of his magnificence. When he stumbles on the rocks at the seaside, he looks to see if he is hurt, then picks himself up and carries on. His perseverance has a joy to it that one does not often see in adults. When we're reading a book about animals, and he mistakenly calls a coral snake a king snake, I correct him, showing him the difference: the coral snake has two yellow stripes flanking a black stripe, the king snake has two black stripes flanking a yellow stripe. He thrives on the error, seizing the right answer the way he seized a rattle or toy car when he was two years younger. And when we tell stories, he corrects me when I confuse characters or accidentally leave out a crucial chase or battle. My imperfections give him a chance to teach me, to show me what he knows. To be imperfect is to grow in knowledge, which is one of the consolations of being human. To think of Nathaniel as perfect, to define him as a spiritual idea, would be to interpose a shadow between us and diminish the pleasure we take in each other's reality. It may be that Nathaniel is made in the image and likeness of God, but as we learn from each other and grow in each other's presence, God grows with us, an antidote to the divinity I once sought so desperately.

When Nathaniel was born, in a room looking out on the Pacific coastal range from the Stanford University Medical Center, he arrived with panache: he left Lesley's body with some velocity, arriving all at once several inches down the bed. He came with open eyes; even our earliest pictures of him, taken a few seconds after he was born, show him wide-eyed and slightly shocked.

After about five minutes, as Nathaniel lay in the warm bassinet, the nurse turned away to find another blanket for him. He suddenly grabbed the top edge of the bassinet with his right hand, pulled hard, and managed to launch himself over the side. The nurse, the attending pediatrician, and I all turned at once, but the nurse got there first; she caught him in mid-air. "Never saw anything like that before," she muttered. We all smiled in relief, wondering who this child would turn out to be.

Nathaniel was never much interested in food; he did not nurse well, and by the sixth week of his life Lesley and I had added infant formula to his diet in an attempt to keep him from falling through the statistical cellar of his age group. After that he grew well, and in four years he has become more clearly the child he was at birth: sharp-eyed, attentive to detail, a careful risk-taker who every now and then launches himself into the unknown, a light sleeper, a light eater. And yet he has moved beyond these essential traits. His imagination, as fertile and changeable as a finely wrought story, regularly brings him into battle with the assorted forces of evil. His knowledge of witches, for example, comes from Disney rather than Margot Adler, but he insistently distinguishes between good witches—who use their powers to help others—and bad witches—who inflict suffering and use their powers to make themselves strong and frightening. He sees himself even now as a defender, as someone who battles the powerful for the sake of the meek.

When Nathaniel was our only child, I sometimes slipped into the fallacy of thinking of all children in terms of him. It struck me that all children might be basically alike, sharing some kind of spiritual link which I dimly envisioned even as I avoided the language of my former religion. Georgia has disabused me of that notion. From the moment of her arrival she was innately different from her brother. As she emerged after a brief labor (as opposed to Lesley's twelve-hour labor with Nathaniel), she eased her way into the world, passing up the chance for a bold flop onto the bed. Preferring to keep her eyes closed, she did not begin a regular routine of looking around for several days. On the other hand, she nursed well and ate hungrily from the beginning. She also slept remarkably well for a newborn, giving us three or four hours of uninterrupted sleep a night. She is a quieter child than Nathaniel was, more attuned to bodily rhythms and more mellow, but when her temper flares it seems clear that she has been blessed with a combined dose of family tempers. I hope this will be a useful trait, as it is for Nathaniel: if all goes well, she will be able to say what she thinks without fear.

How strange it is to see children, from the moment of birth enmeshed in their own rhythms and nascent identities, fundamentally separate from the psyches and wills of the parents! And yet, of course, the influence of those parental psyches and wills is enormous. I find myself hoping that Nathaniel and Georgia will in some ways take after my brother and sister, who trusted their instincts enough to rebel when the world in which they lived seemed false to them. And I hope that Lesley and I will be less like my parents, who saw rebellion as a threat to their own anxious authority and sought to suppress it rather than to learn from it.

One cannot easily predict one's own failings and blindness, yet the will to do so is—I hope—a sign of blessed imperfection, in which love and knowledge mingle in a volatile combination. The ensuing explosions, the misunderstandings and furies and blessings, may be frightening, but cannot be evaded. They are the raw, inelegant evidence that God is with us.

This evening, as Georgia sleeps quietly with Lesley in my sister's house, Nathaniel and I have gone into the woods to search for wicked witches. I am an honorary good witch. The quest begins with a search for the right magic sticks, which must be fairly straight and long. Nathaniel looks patiently, rejecting most of the samples his more impatient father offers him. If the magic is to work, the sticks must be just right. After several minutes of looking, he finds two that suit him; he gives one to me.

"If you see wicked witches, you tell me," he says wisely, "and wave the stick at them and yell. They'll go 'poof!' Then all the deer will be safe."

We sight several witches as we move back through the woods toward the road. Some of these I spot first, while Nathaniel gets the others. In the gathering darkness of night any remnant shadow is a good target. At the road's edge, we congratulate each other on vanquishing such dangerous foes. The islanders are building a new school just down the road, so we head that way to play on the bulldozer and steam shovel. Then Nathaniel freezes, a fraction of a second before I see why: three deer have emerged from the forest gloom a scant hundred feet away. Upwind from us, they cannot catch our scent but know that we are there; they stand, uncertain, watching. We watch. Nathaniel smiles, and I realize that he is proud of himself. He has saved these deer from spell-casting predators. We move closer slowly. Suddenly the buck, confused, begins to run directly at us. Nathaniel and I freeze again; it is our turn to be uncertain. I step in front of my son, acting on instinct, and charge the buck. Catching my scent, he swerves to the left, stops, then turns and runs back into the woods. The others follow him.

On the bulldozer, fiddling with levers and switches, we talk about the deer. "What were their names?" I ask Nathaniel.

"Deer and Here and Near," he says confidently, an archetypal namer.

"Did the big one frighten you?" I ask.

"A little," he says. "But he wasn't going to hurt me."

"How do you know?" I ask.

Nathaniel doesn't answer; he knows. My adult mind immediately raises questions: is this a kind of faith that Nathaniel has, or is it knowledge? Did he trust in his safety the way I, as a Christian Science child, tried to trust in God? The motions of every human life seem to raise more or less the same questions about faith and knowledge and love, but those seem too abstract or transparent tonight. What we have done is concrete: we have walked in the woods, found sticks, dispersed witches, seen and named the deer.

A SUMMER STORM HAS SETTLED IN, WITH ITS FULL COMPLEMENT of rain and fog. I have come down to the harbor. One of the two main island anchorages, this harbor is long and relatively skinny, perhaps a half mile wide; it is one of the more protected Maine berths, its mouth almost sealed by a large, half-wild island called, in the taciturn Maine vernacular, Harbor Island. This natural citadel permits only two narrow entrances to the harbor—the Western Way, a largely unobstructed channel, and the eastern passage, a tricky bit of water dotted with shoals and proto-islands. In the fog, of course, these are largely irrelevant details, because no one can move without radar: a good Maine fog obliterates anything more than a hundred feet from where you stand. Even inveterate radar sailors rarely attempt the harbor in such weather, because disaster may rest on a slight miscalculation. Today the lobster fleet rides its moorings; although from the dock I can only see one or two of the boats, I read from their presence a larger fact. A ghostly sloop turns with the tide at the edge of my sight.

I have come down to row. No one is around today; the wharf is deserted. I climb down the old wooden ladder to the floating dock where my sister keeps her seven-foot dinghy. The storm at sea has blown in the usual sea crud, the flotsam of old Clorox bottles and tennis shoes and seaweed. The surface of the water is a little oily, and eerily smooth. From around the harbor muted sounds mingle with each other at some distant, indeterminate point. A chain saw strikes wood somewhere; someone laughs; a diesel engine under repair turns over once or twice. Untying the generic knot at the bow of the dinghy, I toss the bowline into the bow, slide the boat off the dock, set the oars in their oarlocks, and shove off.

For a few minutes I simply float. The tide is going out, pulling the dinghy slowly into the center of the fishing fleet. Boats appear as if from nowhere, luminescent at first—what one might imagine a spirit to be. In an instant they become solid, isolated objects. Although I have never loved sport rowing, the kind that requires long oars and narrow sculls, I love to row rowboats. The urge goes back to my days of sailing in Avalon. A sunny day on this island will often find me well out of the harbor in the Western Way, heading for the far buoy in swells as high as my gunwales. But these rows have almost nothing in common with a journey through the fog. I take up my oars, give up on drifting for awhile. This is what I love.

Instantly, almost without intention, my body goes on alert: half robbed of sight, I make up for the loss like any wounded person, whose other senses become more acute. That slight slap off to port—a small wave on the hull of a ship, or a rocky shoal? I stare as if my eyes could penetrate the fog, knowing they cannot, knowing they will be sufficient. The faintest trace of a dark horizontal line—a hull waterline—comes into view. Good. Recalling the location of this lobster boat from yesterday's row, I mark my position on the rough map in my mind—directly across from the fishermen's co-op, about halfway down the harbor and just to the right of the channel.

Listening, sensing my bearings as I move from boat to boat, I come to the place where there are no more boats. I have passed the moorings. The water now acquires motion: swells and a light chop overtake the eerie stillness. I know now that I am in the Western Way. But where? The lighthouse is invisible, the foghorn out of order. Now it is time to creep. There is a green bell buoy out here somewhere: listen for the slightest scrape of the bell in these easy seas. There it is, more or less where I expected. The fog plays tricks on one's ears, of course, and yet locations are not unfigurable. I look at where I have come. The oars have made little eddies in the water behind me; although the fog has grown thicker, my wake is straight for the fifty feet that I can see astern. If I'm wrong—if somehow I have made a gradual turn to star-board—then my next spate of rowing may carry me out to sea. On the other hand, my wake and this bell buoy suggest that I am on course, and that if I continue I will reach Harbor Island in a few minutes.

This is always the moment of doubt. What am I doing out here? I pause for a moment, holding the oars just off the water, drifting slightly to starboard to see what it feels like. The swells grow a little larger: clearly I am in mid-channel now. I hear only my breathing, and the slight slap of my oars in the water. I listen anyway, sure with the confidence of a well-tutored heart that I will hear the sound of small waves on a shore at any time. A long time seems to go by; could I have been wrong? With each stroke my hearing seems to grow keener; my head aches slightly from the concentration. And then, confirming my hope and knowledge, I catch the sound of waves on solid ground. In a few more minutes I have dragged the dinghy up onto the pebbly beach of Harbor Is-land, and as I look toward what I take to be the larger island I find that, predictably, I can see nothing: I could be in the middle of the ocean, or the middle of nowhere.

My adult conscience, quieted through this ordeal of keen senses, leaps back into action. What have I accomplished with this little escapade? I laugh, a little ruefully; the sound gets lost in the pines surrounding me. I have accomplished noth-ing, I have made no mark on the world, I have not mastered a new technique of navigation or added to the world's store of knowledge. I have, for the time being, simply lived. And in this moment of life, trusting the totality of my senses and judgment, I have once again noted God's absence, as I do in the air or on a motorcycle. It is a comforting absence. But it does not make God meaningless. His meaning lies in the fog, in my fear of being lost, in my counter-intuition that I do, in fact, know where I am and can find my way.

And, in the end, there are destinations, islands appearing out of the fog first as shades and then as hard, definite realities—not spiritual but physical, yet with the trace of spirit that comes from being concealed or, for a time, unknown. This row has not been a metaphor for my life and faith; it has been my life and faith.

The Father-Mother God, which kind people offered me so many years ago as a metaphor arising from the most concrete source in my life, has been sheered away: it was always false. Yet the power of love and knowledge, which lay dormant in that conception of God, surged into the vacuum that all powerful metaphors leave. In that love and knowledge I found life—amorphous at first, without bearings, frightening, and yet insistent. Choosing, I set out into the fog, and trusted in a divine voice so unlike anything I had ever heard before that it seemed an absence.

Shoving off from Harbor Island, rowing strongly, I pass what I cannot see: the shoals near the lighthouse, the new lobster pound, the hauling-up place in a nook of the harbor. I pull way out to starboard, knowing that I am passing up my chance to navigate from boat to boat. I row by smell. The slightly warm fragrance of grass and earth means that I am near the far shore, and as I look down into the water I realize I can see the bottom; on this low tide I have approached the shoals across from the fishermen's co-op. With a hard turn to port I head again into the gray blindness, catching sight of the white lobster boat near my sister's small sloop *Ishmael,* and then *Ishmael* itself; from the sloop a westerly course, which I read from the compass in my mind, will take me to the dock.

For so many years I was running blind and deaf, talking back to the world in a religious language as it spoke to me in my own language and revealed itself to me in simple, straightforward images—in toys and travels, in adventures, in bodies. Perhaps it was a blessed blindness, though the cost was high: was it necessary to endure so much pain, to see nothing with such clear sight?

Looking out over the invisible harbor, I begin to understand how to come to terms with that question. I have always traveled blind, crossing from here to there in a fog that ought to have kept me tightly locked in the small prisons of my imagination. Yet a voice somewhere within still said go! despite the evident impossibilities of the journey; and islands disappeared and appeared along the way—though not always when I needed them. To spin a web of perfection around this voyage is to consent to blindness; to embrace the imperfection is to gain a glimmer of light.

Turning toward that invisible, luminous source, I hear a child's voice speaking some of the first words I learned from *Science and Health*: " 'To those leaning on the sustaining Infinite,' " the small voice cries, " 'to-day is big with blessings.' " Abandoning the sustaining Infinite here on this dock, I look toward the finite sustenance of a long journey, and know that my survival depends, as it always has, on the naked God who sings to me.